The New Americans
Recent Immigration and American Society

Edited by
Steven J. Gold and Rubén G. Rumbaut

A Series from LFB Scholarly

Health and Behavior among Immigrant Youth

Hayley A. Hamilton

LFB Scholarly Publishing LLC
New York 2005

Library of Congress Cataloging-in-Publication Data

Hamilton, Hayley A., 1966-
  Health and behavior among immigrant youth / Hayley A. Hamilton.
    p. cm. -- (The new Americans)
  Includes bibliographical references and index.
  ISBN 1-59332-097-3 (alk. paper)
  1. Teenage immigrants--United States--Health and hygiene 2. Teenage immigrants--United States--Mental health. 3. Teenage immigrants--United States--Social conditions. I. Title. II. Series: New Americans (LFB Scholarly Publishing LLC)
  RJ102.H35 2005
  362.198'92'000973--dc22

2005022512

ISBN 1-59332-097-3

Printed on acid-free 250-year-life paper.

Manufactured in the United States of America.

Table of Contents

List of Tables vii

List of Figures ix

Acknowledgements xi

Chapter 1: Introduction 1

Chapter 2: Overview of Literature 7

Chapter 3: Data and Measures 31

Chapter 4: Health and Behavior 47

Chapter 5: Family Process 65

Chapter 6: Mental Health and Behavior...................... 83

Chapter 7: Physical Health 101

Chapter 8: Conclusion 119

Appendix 131

Notes 143

References 145

Index 159

List of Tables

4.1. Depressive Symptoms Regressed on Immigrant
    Generation 50

4.2. Positive Affect Regressed on Immigrant Generation 52

4.3. Deviant Behavior Regressed on Immigrant Generation 54

4.4. Physiological Stress Response Regressed on
    Immigrant Generation 56

4.5. Ordered Logit of School Absence Due to Illness on
    Immigrant Generation 58

4.6. Overall Health Regressed on Immigrant Generation 60

5.1. Independence in Decision-Making Regressed on
    Immigrant Generation 68

5.2. Parental Expectation for Education Regressed on
    Immigrant Generation 70

5.3. Parent-Child Closeness Regressed on Immigrant
    Generation 72

5.4. Logistic Regression of Parent-Child Conflict on
    Immigrant Generation 74

5.5. Parental Involvement Regressed on Immigrant
    Generation 76

5.6. Social Support Regressed on Immigrant Generation 78

6.1. Depressive Symptoms Regressed on Generation
    and Family Process 90

6.2. Positive Affect Regressed on Generation
      and Family Process 94

6.3. Deviant Behavior Regressed on Generation
      and Family Process 97

7.1. Physiological Stress Response Regressed on
      Generation and Family Process 105

7.2. School Absence Due to Illness Regressed on
      Generation and Family Process 108

7.3. Overall Health Regressed on Generation
      and Family Process 114

A.1. Weighted Means, Proportions and Standard Deviations 132

A.2. Correlation of Control and Predictor Variables
      with Immigrant Generation and Family Process 134

A.3. Weighted Means and Proportions by Immigrant
      Generation 137

A.4. Weighted Means of Family Process and Well-
      Being Measures by Ethnicity and Immigrant Generation 139

List of Figures

6.1. Depressive Symptoms by Parent-Child Closeness and
Immigrant Generation 91

6.2. Depressive Symptoms by Parental Education and
Immigrant Generation 92

6.3. Positive Affect by Parent-Child Closeness and
Immigrant Generation 95

6.4. Positive Affect by Ethnicity and Immigrant Generation 96

6.5. Deviant Behavior by Sex and Immigrant Generation 98

6.6. Deviant Behavior by Ethnicity and Immigrant Generation 99

7.1. Physiological Stress Response by Household Income
and Immigrant Generation 106

7.2a. Probability of No Absences by Parent-Child Conflict and
Immigrant Generation 111

7.2b. Probability of Few Absences by Parent-Child Conflict
and Immigrant Generation 111

7.3a. Probability of No Absences by Expectations for
Education and Immigrant Generation 112

7.3b. Probability of Few Absences by Expectations for
Education and Immigrant Generation 113

7.4. Overall Health by Ethnicity and Immigrant Generation 116

Acknowledgements

I am grateful to John Mirowsky, Elizabeth Cooksey, and James Moody for their intellectual support throughout this study. This research uses data from Add Health, a program project designed by J. Richard Udry, Peter S. Bearman, and Kathleen Mullan Harris, and funded by a grant P01-HD31921 from the National Institute of Child Health and Human Development, with cooperative funding from 17 other agencies. Special acknowledgment is due Ronald R. Rindfuss and Barbara Entwisle for assistance in the original design. Persons interested in obtaining data files from Add Health should contact Add Health, Carolina Population Center, 123 W. Franklin Street, Chapel Hill, NC 27516-2524 (www.cpc.unc.edu/addhealth/contract.html).

CHAPTER 1

Introduction

The increasing number and diversity of immigrants to the United States over the past few decades has given rise to questions about their health and well-being relative to their American-born counterparts. There are several reasons to expect that the health of foreign-born children would be worse than that of native-born American children. First, families tend to immigrate to the United States to improve their economic circumstances and to escape oppressive political situations. Many have had to live in impoverished and/or chaotic social conditions. Second, in deciding to migrate, family members have to cope with the stress of the migration process as well as adaptation to a new land, culture, and often language. Given such factors, elevated health problems that resolve or improve the longer foreign-born individuals remain in the U.S. would not be surprising. Recent research, however, indicates that the actual health pattern is often the opposite. Newly arrived immigrant children appear to be healthier, on average, than native-born peers and their health appears to worsen the longer they reside in the U.S. (Harris 1999; Hernandez and Charney 1998; Rumbaut 1994a).

This study addresses the discord between intuitive expectations and actual research findings with regard to the health and behavior of foreign-born youth. Of interest are the mechanisms that may explain findings of significant differences in health and behavior between foreign-born and native-born youth. The central question is: Do factors related to family process (e.g., parent-child closeness and conflict) and social support help to explain differences between foreign-born and native-born youth? This question will be addressed by first examining whether immigrant generation is related to health and behavioral outcomes as well as family process and social support. After examining these associations, the role of family process and social support has mediators in the relationship between immigrant generation and health will be assessed.

IMMIGRATION TRENDS

Figures for the year 2003 indicate that the immigrant population is at an all time high, a total of 33.5 million foreign-born persons (Larsen 2004). Although the number is at an all time high, the proportion of the U.S. population that this number represents, 11.7 percent, is less than the high of 14.7 percent foreign-born reported in 1910, but greater than the low of 4.7 percent foreign-born reported in 1970. Immigration figures also indicate that one-half of the foreign-born population in 2003 entered the U.S. since 1990. Of the foreign-born, 13.6 percent immigrated to the U.S. since 2000, 36.6 percent immigrated in the 1990s, 24 percent in the 1980s, 13.7 percent in the 1970s, and the remaining 12.2 percent entered the U.S. before 1970 (Larsen 2004; Lollock 2001; Schmidley and Gibson 1999).

In addition to increasing numbers of immigrants, there is also considerable diversity. Differences in the national origin of older versus more recent immigrants are illustrated by figures indicating that persons from Latin America and the Caribbean represent the largest immigrant population in the United States. Figures for the year 2003 indicate that 53 percent of the foreign-born were born in Latin America, 25 percent were born in Asia, 13.7 percent were born in Europe, and 8 percent were born in other regions of the world (Larsen 2004). Prior to 1990, Europeans made up the largest immigrant group. Today, Filipinos and Mexicans make up the largest Asian and Hispanic immigrant groups, respectively, with Mexicans accounting for more than one-quarter of the foreign-born in the country (Schmidley and Gibson 1999; Rumbaut 1994a; Rumbaut 1994b).

There are also important differences related to class between the foreign-born and native-born population. The foreign-born are less likely to be high school graduates; however, there are no differences with regard to college education between the foreign- and native-born. The foreign-born are also more likely to be unemployed, have less earnings, and live in poverty than the native-born (Larsen 2004). There is also diversity in class among recent immigrants. Recent immigrants are made up of the most as well as the least educated; for example, immigrants from South Asia comprise the most educated group, and those from Mexico are the least educated (Hernandez 2004). Recent immigrants also include the groups with the highest and lowest poverty rates in American society; for example, the foreign-born from Europe and Asia have the lowest poverty rate, and Latin Americans, particularly those from Central America, have the highest (Larsen 2004; Schmidley 2001).

Prior to the 1950s, the majority of immigrants were Italians, Poles, Greeks, Russian Jews, and other "white ethnics". White immigrants, however, declined from 88 percent of arrivals prior to 1960, to 64 percent in the 1960s, 41 percent in the 1970s, 38 percent in the 1980s, and 26 percent in the 1990s. The proportion of black immigrants increased from two percent of arrivals prior to 1960 to eight percent in the 1990s. Asian arrivals increased from five percent prior to 1960 to approximately 25 percent in the 1980s (Rumbaut 1994a; Rumbaut 1994b). The proportion of immigrants from Latin America increased from nine percent in 1960 to 19 percent in 1970, 33 percent in 1980, 44 percent in 1990, and 53 percent in 2003 (Larsen 2004; Schmidley and Gibson 1999).

Another significant aspect of today's immigrants is their tendency to reside in particular regions, states, and cities. This geographic concentration makes their effects particularly pronounced. Approximately 37 percent of today's immigrants reside in the West compared to 29 percent in the South, 22 percent in the Northeast, and 11 percent in the Midwest. Among the native-born, 37 percent reside in the South, 21 percent in the West, 24 percent in the Midwest, and 19 percent in the Northeast (Larsen 2004). States with the highest proportion of immigrants are California, New York, and Florida, in descending order. Immigrants are also more likely to live in metropolitan areas. In 2003, 44 percent of the foreign-born lived in a major city in a metropolitan area, compared with 27 percent of the native-born population (Larsen 2004).

MIGRATION OUTCOMES FOR YOUTH
Much of the discussion on, and research interest in, migration has focused on adults; however, understanding the impact of immigration on children and, particularly adolescents, is very important. Foreign-born children and U.S.-born children with immigrant parents account for almost 20 percent of American children (compared to six percent in 1970) and represent the fastest growing portion of the U.S. child

population. Additionally, these children represent a larger proportion of secondary than elementary school students (Fix and Passel 2003). The fate of these children will determine the long-term effects of contemporary immigration to a much greater extent than the fate of their parents (Rumbaut 1999) as these youth will have a considerable effect on the future of this country. Contemporary immigration will be judged on whether they succeed or fail.

The adolescent years are an important stage of the life course and may be particularly dramatic for the foreign-born. During these years, individuals are not only still undergoing development and socialization phases, they are also in the process of constructing a social identity. That adolescent immigrants also have the burden of assimilating into American society makes their adolescent years more precarious than those of other adolescents. While immigrant adolescents are striving to be less conspicuous than other adolescents and to be accepted by the majority, they are also forced to contend with individuals in the family or community who are focused on either slowing down or aiding the assimilation process through the influence of community peers (Harris 1999); hence, the adaptation process for adolescents often occurs in social contexts that are contradictory (Rumbaut 1994a).

LIMITATIONS OF PREVIOUS STUDIES
The existing research on immigrant youth is limited in several ways. One of the major limitations of previous studies is their lack of generalizability. The lack of good national databases, until recently, to study immigrant youth meant that much of the research to date is based on samples from states with large immigrant populations such as California and Florida. Immigrant populations in other regions of the country deserve study as well to determine if their experiences are similar to those in the more populated regions. Additionally, a large proportion of work is qualitative; thus restricting the generalizability of the results (Padilla and Durán 1995).

A second limitation is that many researchers focus on just one ethnic group. This is related to the lack of a national database that studies immigrants and the limited focus of existing studies. This restricts the level of comparison that can be made in larger discussions of immigrant adaptation and outcomes. A third limitation is the high focus on first-generation immigrants. This focus has meant that the dynamics of the immigration process is less well understood from an intergenerational perspective. A fourth limitation is that much recent research on immigrant children and youth has focused on academic outcomes (Orozco and Todorova 2003; Fuligni 1997). Although education is an important component of successful adaptation, health is also important.

A fifth limitation is that not much is known about the mechanisms through which findings of a health advantage for immigrants arise. Only limited research has been done on the effect of family and neighborhood context on outcomes for immigrant youth (e.g., Harris 1999; Rumbaut 1994a). Again, this limitation is related to the scarcity of available data that could provide answers. The question of how family process and social support might impact health and behavioral outcomes has rarely been examined. The focus of this study on family process, such as adolescents' level of independence in decision-making as a component of adolescent autonomy and parenting style, will thus contribute to the literature.

IMPLICATIONS

The results of this study may have important implications for research, public policy, and clinical practice. The research findings will contribute to the currently small knowledge base on immigrant youth and will provide directions for future research. In trying to explain the association between immigrant status and health and behavior, this study will provide important information about immigrants that further research can build upon. In addition, the study addresses whether the factors that have been found to explain health status for the general population of youth are the same for immigrant youth.

The findings may also have policy implications by helping to educate the public regarding the advantages that immigrants and their children bring to the U.S. So much attention is focused on the negative aspects of immigration (e.g., low English language proficiency) that the potential positive contributions of these youth to the future of the country are lost. If foreign-born youth are in better health, for example, fewer dollars have to be devoted to their health care. Further, if foreign-born youth engage in fewer problem behaviors, fewer dollars have to be spent on their punishment and rehabilitation or counselling.

Knowledge of why foreign-born youth are in better health may be of importance to physical and, particularly, mental health treatment and prevention. Knowing that the factors that contribute to mental illness among immigrant youth are the same or different from those that much research has shown affect the mental health of youth in general, for example, will be of interest to mental health providers. As the number of immigrant youth in the population increases, mental health providers have begun to express concerns about identifying and treating immigrant youth given differences in "culture" which they do not understand.

OUTLINE

The main research question is: Do factors related to family process and social support help to explain any association between adolescent immigrant generation status and health and behavioral outcomes? Before addressing this research question, two relationships are examined: (1) the association between adolescent immigrant generation status and health and behavioral outcomes; and (2) the association between immigrant generation and family process.

The next chapter, Chapter 2, reviews the main theories of immigrant adaptation and discusses the relationship between immigration and health and behavioral outcomes. Chapter 3 outlines the data and measures on which the analyses are based and provide an overview of the analytic strategy. Chapter 4 examines the association between adolescent immigrant generation status and health and behavioral outcomes. Chapter 5 examines the association between adolescent immigrant generation status and family process. Chapters 6 and 7 examine whether or not family process helps to explain the association between immigrant generation and health and behavior. Chapter 8, the final chapter, summarizes the results, discusses the broader implications and limitations of the study, and offers suggestions for future research.

CHAPTER 2

Overview of Literature

Much of the past research on immigrant adaptation has focused on adults. This is reflected in the theoretical explanations for adaptation that are dominant in the literature. The general lack of theoretical frameworks to understand the adaptation of immigrant children, specifically, may be a reflection of more recent interest in this population. Aspects of the dominant theories, however, are relevant to immigrant children. This research will be framed within more general theories of immigrant adaptation.

THEORETICAL BACKGROUND
Assimilation Theory
Classical assimilation theory has been the dominant perspective for much of the past century. The main assumption of the assimilation perspective is that the process through which various ethnic groups end up sharing a common culture and gaining equal access to opportunities is a natural one. That once the process of abandoning old cultures and behaviors in favor of new ones (those of the host country) begins, it invariably and irreversibly leads to assimilation (Warner and Srole 1945; Park 1928). The assimilation process allows immigrants to lose their distinctiveness and blend into mainstream America. Blending into the mainstream requires progression through several stages such as acculturation or cultural assimilation, structural assimilation or intermarriage, and identificational assimilation whereby immigrants develop a self-image as an unhyphenated American (Gordon 1964). In Gordon's view, acculturation, the process whereby immigrants

relinquish old cultures, is a necessary first step in the assimilation process; however, cultural assimilation does not necessarily lead to other forms of integration into the host society. Individuals or groups may not be full social participants in the host society and its institutions. The extent to which ethnic groups remain distinct from each other would largely depend on the extent to which the dominant group accepts particular ethnic groups. Nevertheless, Gordon believed that the distinctive characteristics of ethnic minorities (e.g., old cultural attributes, native languages, ethnic enclaves) would disappear as immigrants progress through the assimilation stages and that this would eventually lead to intermarriage with the majority population and participation in its institutions on a basic level (Gordon 1964). The assimilation perspective considers distinctive traits to be handicaps that are detrimental to assimilation (Warner and Srole 1945; Child 1943); traits that must be discarded to attain upward mobility.

Assimilation may be conceptualized as an intragenerational as well as an intergenerational process. In the former, longer residence in the U.S. leads to a reduction in differences between immigrants and the native-born population. In the latter, the Americanization of immigrants occurs across generations with each subsequent generation being more mainstream than the last (Harris 1999). The assimilation process should be more or less complete by the third generation (Rumbaut 1997b). Many of the immigrants who arrived in the United States, primarily from Europe, in the first half of the 1900s seemed to have been successfully assimilated into American society. For example, research studies on educational attainment, English proficiency, job skills, and exposure to American cultures have indicated progressive trends of social mobility across immigrant generations and increasing rates of intermarriage (Alba 1985; Chiswick 1977; Greeley 1976; Sandberg 1974; Wytrwal 1961).

Segmented Assimilation
Despite findings of increased mobility among European immigrants, the classical theory of assimilation has been much criticized because of a failure to address the complexities of the assimilation process and the multiple pathways to assimilation (Portes 1995; Portes and Böröcz 1989). These criticisms are based on the inability of the assimilation perspective to explain the adaptation of more recently arrived non-European immigrants, especially those from Asia and Latin America. These non-European immigrants have experienced persistent ethnic

differences across generations, a decline in the well-being of the second-generation relative to the first-generation (often referred to as the second-generation decline), and inconsistent outcomes across ethnic groups and individual members (Zhou 1997; Gans 1992; Hirschman and Falcón 1985).

The divergent outcomes among second-generation immigrants form the basis of another framework for understanding immigrant adaptation, the segmented assimilation perspective. Segmented assimilation theory argues that the relatively uniform mainstream America to which immigrants became adapted and integrated 50 years ago has disappeared. The assimilation process has become segmented such that the adaptation process experienced by today's new generation of immigrants may differ depending on the social and economic characteristics of the segment of the American population to which they assimilate (Portes and Zhou 1993). Thus, longer residence in the United States may be associated with mixed outcomes, rather than the automatic social and economic advancement predicted by classic assimilation theory.

The segmented assimilation perspective identifies three distinct forms of adaptation: (1) that which replicates the classical assimilation theory in which longer residence is associated with greater integration into the white middle-class; (2) an adaptation downward into permanent poverty and integration into the underclass, the direct opposite of the classical theory; and (3) an adaptation that involves economic advancement within a strong ethnic community while preserving the values and unity of that immigrant community (Portes and Zhou 1993). The segmented assimilation perspective recognizes that the segment of society in which today's immigrants are received varies from affluent middle-class neighborhoods to poor inner-city ghettos. Given this diversity in the receiving communities, paths to social mobility may lead upward or downward or, for many who were received into poor neighborhoods, nowhere at all (Zhou 1997).

An important question within the segmented assimilation perspective is what factors place some immigrant groups on a downward path to adaptation and others on an upward one? Two types of factors are emphasized, those external to a specific immigrant group and those that are internal to the group. External factors include racial stratification, spatial segregation, and economic opportunities. Factors intrinsic to the group include family structure, human and financial capital upon arrival, cultural patterns of social relations, and community organization (Zhou 1997). Discrimination against immigrants who are visible minorities coupled with changing labor markets, for example, may create barriers to economic advancement and the achievement of aspirations among second-generation youth (Portes 1997). Not only may these youth be denied opportunities to work, they themselves may be reluctant to work for the low wages that their parents did, although they lack the opportunities and skills to do better. The latter phenomenon has been referred to as the second-generation revolt (Perlman and Waldinger 1996 cf. Zhou 1997). Zhou and Bankston (1994) also show how generational role reversal, whereby children of immigrants become their parents' parents because of their greater familiarity with the new language and culture, contribute to downward assimilation among Vietnamese-American children. The main reason for this is that role reversal undermines parental authority over youth at an important stage of development and at a time when youth are exposed to alternative cultures and role models. Of course, particular patterns of family and community relations may sometimes counter trends toward downward assimilation. When immigrant children are being pressured to assimilate, but are unsure which route to take, the family or ethnic community may be able to mobilize resources to avert downward assimilation (Zhou 1997).

Overall, the segmented assimilation perspective argues that whether or not the adaptation process is on an upward or downward route appears to be dependent on individual and family characteristics as well as the circumstances and issues that immigrants encounter upon their arrival. Such issues include those related to race, location of residence, and employment (Portes 1995).

Other Theories
Whereas classical assimilation theory represents a unidimensional or linear view of adaptation, segmented assimilation reflects a more diverse approach that is common in more recent conceptualizations of adaptation. Inherent in the latter approach is the idea that biculturalism, or living with aspects of two cultures (the native and host cultures), is not only common, but may be beneficial to individuals (LaFromboise, Coleman and Gerton 1993; Johnson, Jobe, O'Rourke, et al. 1997; Burnam et al. 1987). Berry noted four diverse ways in which acculturation can occur that distinguishes between assimilation and integration and between separation and marginalization. Berry (1980,

1970) also noted that the attitudes and behaviors that are displayed during routine encounters with other cultures define acculturative strategies. Research has found behavior problems among a greater proportion of children who reject their original culture in favor of that of the larger society (assimilation) compared to children who retain their original culture while accepting that of the larger society (integration) (Pawliuk, Grizenko, Chan-Yip, et al. 1996). There is an acknowledgement in the multidimensional approach that immigrants have many options for interacting within the host culture (Trimble 2003).

Relevance of Theories
Most theories related to acculturation were developed to explain adult adaptation. It has been argued that straight-line assimilation theory, for example, can only be truly tested on second- and later-generation adults (Gans 1999). Attempts to draw conclusions about assimilation theory from studies of a child or youth population would thus be viewed with caution.

The objective of this study is not to prove or disprove unidimensional or multidimensional perspectives, but rather to determine some of the factors that may protect immigrant youth and contribute to positive health and behavioral outcomes. The theories are important, however, because they outline paths to immigrant adaptation. Immigrant children and youth are on these paths even if the success or failure of adaptation cannot be truly determined until their children and grandchildren are adults.

Researchers' knowledge of these theories and research findings that foreign-born children are often in better circumstances with regard to factors such as health, education, and risk behaviors than other children, have triggered increased interest in theories of adaptation and their applicability to children. Given the classical theory, one would expect that children who have resided in the U.S. longer would be more integrated into the mainstream and thus exhibit behaviors and tendencies more similar to U.S.-born children than foreign-born children who have more recently arrived in the country. One would also expect that third- and later-generation children would be more integrated into the mainstream than second-generation children, who would be more integrated than first-generation children. These outcomes would be expected because they would indicate that children of immigrants are on a path towards successful assimilation. The same would apply to segmented assimilation theory in that one would expect that immigrant children with longer residence in the country may not be in better shape than recent arrivals if much of their American experiences have been in negative environments such as poor neighborhoods and schools. Similarly, children and families who retain elements of their native culture while accepting and participating in aspects of the host culture may be in better health than children and families who do not. Although the theories may not be proved or disproved in the child and youth population, they are the foundation for studies of immigrant children that guide our understanding of health and behavioral outcomes.

IMMIGRATION AND HEALTH
Much of the research on the adaptation of immigrant children focuses on educational outcomes such as academic achievement and aspirations (Orozco and Todorova 2003; Fuligni 1997; Zhou 1997). Such studies reinforce the importance of education to social and economic advancement and the successful adaptation to American life that most immigrants envision. Despite the fact that health may affect the ability of immigrants to learn or interact with the larger society, far fewer studies examine health outcomes among immigrant children. The research literature on the association between immigrant status and health and behavior indicates much ambiguity, but also serves to highlight the importance of examining various outcomes. The importance of diverse outcomes is also highlighted by reports that mental health problems often precede physical health problems among adolescents (Walker and Townsend 1998; Sweeting 1995; Mechanic and Hansell 1987).

Immigration and Mental Health
It is well accepted that moving to a new country can lead to psychological distress. In the early 20th century, the sociological literature on the immigrant experience in the United States tended to emphasize loneliness and alienation. The immigration process was thought to have a negative effect on an individual's happiness, self-esteem, and general sense of identity (Portes and Rumbaut 1996; Burnam, Hough, Karno, Escobar, and Telles 1987). This view was supported by studies of European immigrants that consistently found significant levels of psychological disturbance among first-generation immigrants (Malzberg and Lee 1956; Handlin 1951). In addition, the

rate of suicide among the native-born was less than one-third that of the foreign-born population residing in Chicago in 1930 (Stonequist 1961). Despite these initial negative outcomes, it was generally held that the psychological problems would disappear as immigrants assimilate into American society (Sowell 1981; Warner and Srole 1945).

Early findings of increased psychological disturbance among immigrants were challenged by subsequent research indicating that the association between psychological well-being and immigrant status was affected by characteristics such as age, sex, socioeconomic status and region of the country. The differences between European immigrants and natives found in earlier studies of adults were found to disappear after controlling for such characteristics (Portes and Rumbaut 1996; Malzberg and Lee 1956). Results from studies on immigrant youth, however, remain mixed; for example, some research indicate negligible differences in self-concept between foreign-born and native-born youth (Kao 1999), but other research has indicated fewer symptoms of depression and general psychological distress among foreign-born youth (Harker 2001; Harris 1999; Rumbaut 1997b, 1997c). Still other research findings suggest a higher level of emotional distress among immigrant youth (Kao 1999; Rumbaut 1994a).

Research findings that immigrants may be no more mentally ill than native-borns or that immigrants may actually have better mental health than native-borns with similar demographic characteristics are often surprising. Such findings are unexpected given the generally marginal positions of immigrants in American society. Immigrants are generally less educated, they are poorer, they are clustered in urban areas, they may speak English poorly or not at all, and they may have fewer social ties (Fox, Merwin, and Blank 1995; Rumbaut 1994a; Srole et al. 1978). These factors have all been associated with lower levels of psychological well-being (Patten et al. 1997; Fox et al. 1995; Rumbaut 1994a; Mirowsky and Ross 1989; Boyce 1985). Like other subordinate groups who experience powerlessness and alienation, immigrants would be expected to experience greater psychological problems (Portes and Rumbaut 1996). Instead of lower well-being, however, immigrants are often in better mental health. Better mental health among the foreign-born may be due to the euphoria of being in a new country and being given the opportunity for a better life. Additionally, the family environment and parent-child relationship may be better among the foreign-born; thus, leading to better mental health. The family environment and parent-child relationship may be better because parents are likely to be intent on making sure that their children are doing well given the new country and culture. Research has also found that protective characteristics within immigrant cultures may enhance well-being (Rumbaut 1997a; Guendelman and Abrams 1995; Scribner and Dwyer 1989).

In addition to better mental health among immigrants, there is increasing evidence that over time and across generations, the psychological well-being of immigrants declines rather than improves (Harris 1999; Rumbaut 1997a; Hirschman 1996; Rumbaut 1994a; Gans 1992). Harris (1999) found that first- and second-generation immigrant youth are in better mental health than third- and later-generation white youth. Recent studies of suicide also support a protective influence of immigrant status in that first-generation immigrant youth are at a somewhat lower risk of suicide than third- and later-generation youth (Sorenson and Shen 1996). This is in direct opposition to expectations arising from the classical or straight-line assimilation perspective that immigrant well-being will improve over time.

Several possible explanations have been proposed for findings of decreasing psychological well-being with time in the United States. One explanation is acculturative stress. Acculturative stress is part of the process of adapting to a host country's cultures and social structures (Hernandez and Charney 1998; Coll and Magnuson 1997). Several problems are related to acculturative stress. One such problem is language difficulties. Efforts to navigate through a social system can be frustrating if an immigrant's native language is not understood and that individual does not speak the language of his or her host country. A second problem related to acculturative stress is perceived discrimination. Differences between immigrants and native-born that are related to characteristics such as skin color, spoken language, food and eating habits, and clothing may increase the level of discrimination immigrants perceive. A third problem associated with acculturative stress is perceived incompatibilities between the cultures of the country of origin and those of the host country. Such incompatibilities may result from different socialization habits, social roles, family values, and interaction styles. A fourth problem associated with acculturative stress is the increasing gap between the culture that children most associate with and the culture with which their parents feel most affiliated. A likely scenario is one in which parents feel more comfortable with the culture of their country of birth and adhere to the values and norms of that culture; however, their children have greater affiliation for the American culture and adhere to American norms and values (Hernandez and Charney 1998). Acculturative stress may not be experienced immediately upon arrival in a new country; for example, elation over a successful move and the opportunity to start a new life may characterize the first year in the U.S. The second and subsequent years may be considerably more stressful as the impact of language problems, discrimination, and perceived cultural disparities are fully experienced. The manner in which the host community responds to immigrant families is believed to be very important to the psychological well-being of children in such families in subsequent years (Hernandez and Charney 1998). An examination of acculturative stress among Latino adolescent boys found that second- and third- and later-generation youth with low acculturation levels who experience significant language problems, perceived discrimination, and who have little pride in their family are at highest risk for psychological problems (Gil, Vega, and Dimas 1994).

A second explanation for a decline in psychological well-being with time spent in the U.S. or with increasing generation is intergenerational conflict resulting from differential rates of acculturation by parents and children. Immigrant children tend to become Americanized much more swiftly than their parents because their schooling provides them with greater exposure to new norms (Leslie 1993; Baptiste 1993). Children are focused on fitting into American society and parents are often focused on retaining traditional family life (Zhou 1997). These differences in the rates of acculturation may lead to role reversal, especially in instances where parents are not proficient in English and their children have to act as interpreters, loss of parental authority, and increased parent-child conflicts (Buriel and De Ment 1997; Coll and Magnuson 1997; Zhou 1997). Such gaps in the acculturation rate of parents and children have been conceptualized as generational dissonance. Generational consonance arises when parents and children both acculturate at the same rate. They can also both remain unacculturated or decide to engage in selective acculturation whereby they only adopt specific aspects of the new culture (Portes and Rumbaut 1996). Acculturation gaps between immigrant parents and their children have been found to adversely affect children's self-esteem and psychosocial well-being (Gil and Vega 1996; Rumbaut 1994a; Chiu, Feldman, and Rosenthal 1992; Zambrana and Silva-Palacios 1989; Sluzki 1979).

A third explanation for research findings of a decline in psychological well-being across time among the foreign-born is segmented assimilation theory. This perspective views the outcome of immigrant adaptation as dependent on the segment of the population to which the immigrant assimilates. Deterioration in psychological well-being over time and across generations, therefore, may result from immigrant children and children of immigrants assimilating in unfavorable contexts such as areas with poor labor market prospects and high perceived discrimination. The majority of today's second-generation children are faced with such negative contextual factors (Portes and Rumbaut 1996).

Although the assimilation process is often plagued with factors that may be associated with psychological distress, such as intergenerational conflict and acculturative stress, findings of better psychological well-being among new immigrants indicate that they are often not immediately affected. Two possible reasons for new immigrants greater psychological well-being are the excitement over moving to a new country and the knowledge or hope that their lives will be improved (Hernandez and Charney 1998). These can be powerful emotions and it can take a few years for them to feel despair at the reality of life in a new country, especially if that reality is the opposite of what they expected. Additionally, with time, the group against which they compare themselves will likely change. When immigrants first move to the U.S., they likely continue to compare their lives to those of their peers in their homeland. With time and across generations, however, their point of reference will switch to their American peers (Portes and Zhou 1993) and, if they do not consider their lives equal to those of their peers, they may begin to experience distress. This applies to adolescents as well as adults because, although adolescents may be unhappy about leaving their friends, the excitement of moving to the U.S. will likely be present nonetheless.

IMMIGRATION AND PHYSICAL HEALTH

As immigrants assimilate into a new society and adopt new values and norms their physical health status may also undergo changes. In adopting new norms, immigrants may be likely to adopt some of the dominant norms that relate to health behavior. Engaging in health behaviors that are similar to those of the majority group may shift the health status of immigrant groups closer to that of the majority group (Mendoza et al. 1990). In the past, it was generally assumed that in the case of immigrants, a shift in health behaviors would result in positive outcomes. A growing body of research, however, indicates that physical health status does not necessarily improve with time spent in the U.S. or across immigrant generations (Gordon-Larsen, Harris, Ward, and Popkin 2003; Landale, Oropesa, and Gorman 1999; Landale, Oropesa, Llanes, and Gorman 1999; Harris 1999; Guendelman, English, and Chavez 1995; Guendelman and English 1995; Markides and Coreil 1986).

Findings that assimilation does not necessarily translate into better physical health were first identified in studies of low birthweight and infant mortality among the Mexican-born population (Hernandez and Charney 1998; Guendelman et al. 1995; Guendelman and English 1995; Scribner and Dwyer 1989; Williams, Binkin, and Clingman 1986; Markides and Coreil 1986). Despite the low socioeconomic status of Mexican immigrant women, less adequate prenatal care, and a higher proportion of mothers over the age of 35, rates of low birthweight and infant mortality are much lower among these immigrant women than among native-born women. Results from the Hispanic Health and Nutrition Examination Survey (HHANES) have indicated that second-generation Mexican-American women have a rate of low birth weight that is two to four times higher than that of similar first-generation immigrant women (Portes and Rumbaut 1996). This phenomenon is usually referred to as an epidemiological paradox because it is contrary to what would normally be expected (Portes and Rumbaut 1996). Subsequent research identified similar patterns among other ethnic groups (Hernandez and Charney 1998; Collins and Shay 1994; Rumbaut and Weeks 1989). Attempts to explain this phenomenon have not been very successful. Early attempts focused on socioeconomic status and prenatal care; however, the health advantage for immigrant women remained regardless of their socioeconomic status and despite less prenatal care (Landale et al. 1999). Recent and more accepted explanations have focused on the protective influence of immigrants' ethnic culture, such as norms and social support networks. Familism, for example, tends to be greater among immigrants than non-immigrants (Kaplan and Marks 1990). Within some cultures, it is believed that family needs supersede individual needs and close family networks may help with pregnancy needs and promote healthy behaviors (Landale et al. 1999). Research has shown that immigrant women tend to lead healthier lifestyles–they are less likely to smoke during pregnancy, less likely to use alcohol and drugs, and appear to have a healthier diet than native-born women (Landale et al. 1999; Guendelman and Abrams 1995; Cabral, Friend, Levenson, Amaro, and Zuckerman 1990). There is evidence that research findings of a health advantage for the foreign-born may also apply to children and adolescents. Although there is not much existing research in this area, children of immigrants appear to be healthier or as healthy as children in native-born families (Hernandez and Charney 1998). Results from the 1994 National Health Interview Survey (NHIS) indicate that first- and second-generation children and adolescents experience fewer acute and chronic health problems, fewer health problems that limited their everyday activities, and are less likely to miss school or be placed in special classes due to health problems (Hernandez and Charney 1998). Recent research on several general health issues of concern to adolescents is outlined below.

A health issue that has received increasing attention among the general population is obesity. Overweight and obese adolescents have become an increasing public health concern in the U.S. (Troiano, Flegal, Kuzmarski, Campbell and Johnson 1995). Figures indicate that approximately 11 percent of adolescents ages 12 to 17 were overweight between 1988 and 1994 and that twice as many adolescents from poor households were overweight than adolescents from middle and high income households (National Center for Health Statistics 2000). Children and adolescents who are overweight are at increased risk for hypertension, noninsulin-dependent diabetes, gall bladder disease, and a host of other illnesses (Barlow and Dietz 1998; Himes and Dietz 1994). They are also more likely to become overweight adults (Guo, Roche, Chumlea, Gardner, and Siervogel 1994). Foreign-born youth have been found to have similar or lower levels of overweight and obesity than native-born youth. Harris (1999) found less obesity among immigrant youth than their native-born counterparts even after controlling for demographic characteristics and family and neighborhood context. Among Cuban and Puerto Rican youth, increasing overweight has been associated with longer residence in the U.S. (Gordon-Larsen, et al. 2003). An examination of nutritional status using HHANES found that Mexican-born immigrant children are not significantly different from native-born Mexican-Americans with regard to dietary intake, body mass index, and rates of anemia (Mendoza and Dixon 1999). In contrast, smoking, inactivity, and less healthy diet have been found to increase with generation (Gordon-Larsen et al. 2003).

A chronic condition that has risen in frequency in the past few decades is asthma. Asthma is one of the most common chronic conditions experienced by children (Hernandez and Charney 1998). There is considerable variation in its prevalence across ethnic groups. This variation may be due to ethnic differences related to biology, culture, and socioeconomic status although the process is not well understood (Hernandez and Charney 1998). Asthma in children of immigrants may be particularly complicated because the migration process itself may aggravate the condition (e.g., leaving a tropical climate and settling in a temperate one with more varying pollen rates) (Sin et al. 1997; Echechipia et al. 1995). In addition, immigrant families may hold different cultural beliefs about the cause and proper treatment of the condition. Not much is known about the prevalence of asthma in children in immigrant families relative to those in native-born families. A recent study by Harris (1999) found that foreign-born youth experience lower levels of asthma than native-born youth. In an examination of the Mexican-American population, Mendoza and Dixon (1999) found similar rates of chronic condition among foreign-born and native-born youth.

Adolescents' perception of their individual health is also an important component of physical well-being. Despite reports of fewer individual health problems, both immigrant parents and their children have been found to report less favorable overall health (Mendoza and Dixon 1999; Hernandez and Charney 1998). Mendoza and Dixon (1999) found that among Mexican-Americans, foreign-born adolescents are almost twice as likely to perceive their health as poor than are adolescents born in the U.S. Other researchers have indicated that 2.5 times as many youth with foreign-born parents report fair or poor health compared to youth with native-born parents (Capps, Fix, and Reardon-Anderson 2003). Similar results are found in studies where children's overall health is based on parental report. These results seem to indicate that culture may play an important role in people's perception of their own health (Mendoza and Dixon 1999).

Based on the higher levels of health problems among low-income groups and immigrants' propensity to be highly represented among such groups, one would expect health problems to be significantly higher among immigrant children. The findings as outlined above, however, indicate that immigrant children are likely to enjoy a health advantage. This advantage tends to disappear over time as children adopt health risk behaviors more similar to those of the native-born population (Harris 1999). Two possible explanations for these findings are increased exposure to stressors and a reduction in protective factors (Landale et al. 1999). Possible stressors include poverty, perceived discrimination, poor neighborhoods, and generally unfulfilled expectations (Landale et al. 1999). Assimilating into such circumstances tends to result in poor outcomes (Portes and Rumbaut 1996). The reduction in protective factors explanation is based on findings that immigrant cultures have protective characteristics that enhance the well-being of immigrants and their children (Rumbaut 1997a; Guendelman and Abrams 1995; Scribner and Dwyer 1989; Rumbaut and Weeks 1989). Such findings challenge the classical assimilation perspective that immigrants need to forsake their home culture in order to become Americanized and improve their circumstances. The beneficial health practices of immigrant families appear to deteriorate as individuals' adherence to cultural norms decrease (Landale et al. 1999)

PROBLEM BEHAVIORS
During the process of adapting to a new culture, immigrants may change their behavior in order to better conform to the new society. A group of behaviors that is of particular interest is health risk behaviors; that is, behaviors that place adolescents at risk for health problems. Such behaviors have been linked to poor physical and mental health among the general youth population (National Center for Health Statistics 2000; Harris 1999). These findings make recent research showing a relationship between assimilation and risky behaviors particularly noteworthy.

The extent to which children engage in sex, smoke, use drugs and alcohol, and engage in other delinquent acts have been found to vary by immigrant status (Harris 1999; Hernandez and Charney 1998; Brindis, Wolfe, McCarter, Ball, and Starbuck-Morales 1995). Research has indicated elevated use of alcohol, tobacco, and illicit drugs among Hispanic youth who perceive themselves as highly acculturated into American society, or who aspire to be highly acculturated (Brindis et al. 1995). Other research has found that foreign-born children engage in less delinquent and violent behavior. Harris (1999), for example, found that foreign-born youth are much less likely to be delinquent and violent than native-born youth with immigrant parents even after controlling for family context, neighborhood context, and demographic characteristics. Gibson and Ogbu (1991) found that immigrant children report less behavior problems than their native-born counterparts. Additionally, in an examination of adherence to particular cultures, Wong (1999) found that youth of Chinese descent who adhere to Chinese culture are less delinquent than those who adhere to North American culture.

The increase in risky behaviors with increasing time in the U.S. may be a result of immigrants adopting the behaviors, habits, and lifestyles of the American culture (Harris 1999). This is particularly relevant for youth as they are quicker to shed their old culture and adopt the new in their attempt to fit into American society. This is usually accomplished through peers, an influential agent of socialization during the adolescent years (Rumbaut 1994b). Research has found that adolescents who are highly acculturated are more likely to be attached to their peers (Wong 1999). Although the classical assimilation perspective assumed that interacting with more Americanized peers would be advantageous for immigrants, research has shown that this is not necessarily so. Wong (1999) found that highly acculturated adolescents are more likely to associate with delinquent peers. This reinforces the segmented assimilation argument that if immigrants assimilate into negative contexts and if they associate with negative role models then they may assimilate downwards; thus, reducing the likelihood of ever achieving social and economic success.

FAMILY PROCESS
Despite a recent increase in research examining adaptation outcomes for immigrant children and children of immigrants, much remains unknown about the mechanisms through which immigrant status affects outcomes. For example, why might foreign-born youth experience a health advantage over native-born youth? There are many factors that could possibly account for variations in the health and behavior of youth. One such factor is family process or family functioning. There are several reasons for postulating that family process may affect the relationship between immigrant status and health and behavioral outcomes.

The family is one of the most important agents of socialization in children's lives. There is much evidence that family factors are associated with the well-being of children and adolescents. Factors such as parent-child conflict, the level of closeness between parents and children, and parental supervision of children may have protective influences on well-being (Patten et al. 1997; Rumbaut 1994a; Dornbusch 1989; Marjoribanks 1987; Steinberg 1986). The limited research that has examined the family structure and process of immigrant children indicates somewhat similar results. Research, for example, consistently shows better psychological well-being among immigrant children from intact families than among those in single-parent families, and better well-being among those from families with well-developed social networks than among those whose families are socially isolated (Zhou 1997). Family process has also been found to mediate the relationship between poverty and mental health among native-born children (Beiser, Hou, Hyman and Tousignant 2002). Healthy parent-child associations and family ties are important sources of support and control. Although family factors are associated with well-being in many respects, the association may differ for immigrants and non-immigrants given the diversity in parenting styles and the possible diverse influences on children. There are also distinct differences in what might be considered healthy and normative child development, especially between collectivistic and individualistic societies. Several factors involved in parent-child association are outlined below.

Parental supervision serves to monitor and control children's behavior and often leads to greater interaction and communication between parents and children. Greater communication within the family has been linked to greater social skills, higher academic achievement, and more positive attitudes among children (Dornbusch 1989). Research has found that children who are highly supervised are less likely to experience psychological problems, less likely to commit delinquent acts and engage in impulsive behavior, and more likely to succeed academically (Steinberg 1986; Dornbusch et al. 1985). There is little research on the level of parental supervision in immigrant families. A recent study by Harker (2001) found that foreign-born youth experience greater parental supervision than native-born youth.

Autonomy is an important aspect of the relationship between parents and adolescents. As adolescence is often viewed as a transition into adulthood, it is important that adolescents have some freedom to display self-direction (Crockett and Crouter 1995). Research has shown, for example, that adolescents with autonomy from parents have higher self-esteem (Bush 2000). Other research has found that Chinese mothers have a greater tendency to adopt restrictive childrearing practices than Chinese American and European American mothers (Chiu 1987). The age at which adolescents expect autonomy was also found to vary by generation with first-generation Chinese Americans expecting autonomy at a much later age than their second-generation counterparts, and with the second-generation Chinese Americans expecting autonomy at a later age than European-Americans (Feldman and Rosenthal 1990).

Conflict is another aspect of parent-child relations. A frequent issue in parent-child conflict involves parental supervision or lack of autonomy (Collins and Luebker 1994). Research has indicated that parent-child conflict is associated with low self-esteem, depression, behavior problems, and poor school performance (Rumbaut 1997c; Shek 1997). Parent-child conflict may be particularly serious for immigrant parents and their children (Waters 1997; Rumbaut 1994a). In addition to the usual barrage of issues confronted during the adolescent years, immigrant youth are also faced with having to balance two cultures. Immigrant parents may be confronted with having to balance differences in norms related to child discipline between their home and host countries (Waters 1997). In a study of the children of immigrants, Rumbaut (1994a) found that parent-child conflict is less likely to occur in homes with two natural parents and where parents and siblings both provide help with homework. Parent-child conflict is more likely to occur: with daughters; with children who prefer to speak English at home and lack proficiency in the parents' native language; with children who spend many hours watching television and few hours on homework; with children with low academic performance and educational aspirations; with children who feel embarrassed by their parents; with children who have experienced discrimination; and in families with less educated mothers and those that have experienced a decline in their economic circumstances. Results have been inconsistent with regard to the question of whether parent-child conflict is greater among immigrants or the native-born. Although Rumbaut (1994a) found that parent-child conflict appeared more likely to occur among the most recent immigrants, Harker (2001) found less parent-child conflict among immigrant children than among their native-born counterparts.

A high level of closeness between parents and children may be associated with high levels of involvement, with parents and children communicating and engaging in activities together. It may also increase children's perception of parental support and decrease conflict within the home. There is some evidence that adolescents tend to feel close to their parents (Field, Lang, Yando, and Bendell 1995; Steinberg 1991) and that those who do also tend to experience greater psychological well-being (Field et al. 1995; Steinberg 1991; Dornbusch 1989; Greenberg, Siegel, and Leitch 1983). Additionally, feeling close to one's parents tends to moderate the effects of stressful life events on adolescents (Greenberg et al. 1983). There is little research on the level of closeness and involvement between immigrant parents and their children. Findings by Harker (2001) appear to indicate that immigrant children feel less close to their parents.

Although only one aspect of social support, that between parents and children, is directly embedded in parent-child association, the level of general social support perceived may have important influences on child outcomes. Research has found that individuals who perceive high levels of social support from parents, friends, and other adults report better physical and mental health (Wickrama, Lorenz, and Conger 1997; Patten et al. 1997; Zhou 1997; Short and Johnston 1997; Thoits 1995; Vilhjalmsson 1994; Vega, Kolody, Valle, and Weir 1991; Boyce 1985; Cohen and Syme 1985; Mechanic 1980). Perceived social support is particularly important to immigrant children given that the immigrant experience is often a stressful one. The perception of high levels of social support among immigrant children may act as a buffer and protect them from more serious outcomes (Short and Johnston 1997). Research has found that foreign-born youth tend to experience greater social support (Harker 2001).

Healthy parent-child association and family ties are important sources of support and control. Recent research on immigrant families, however, has indicated that family cohesiveness tends to decline with increasing years spent in the United States (Harker 2001; Gil and Vega 1996). Why might family cohesiveness and, specifically, parent-child association deteriorate over time and generations among immigrant families? Normal parent-child relations are almost invariably disrupted due to the migration process itself (Zhou 1997; Sluzki 1979). Additionally, immigrants are often confronted with factors that contribute to acculturative stress and intergenerational conflict. For example, parents' lack of proficiency in English may lead to role reversal with children acting as translators for their parents (Zhou 1997; Coll and Magnuson 1997). In their capacity as translators, children in immigrant families are given much more authority and become much more involved in particular aspects of their parents' lives, aspects in which they would have had no involvement if not for their parents' language difficulties. This may lead to a reduction in parental authority and an increase in parent-child conflict.

Increasing the likelihood of some deterioration in family cohesiveness are the differences between parents' and children's perceptions of American society. Children are anxious that they are not becoming American fast enough. They are focused on the external traits that define an American and struggle to fit in based on a frame of reference obtained through their native-born peers and the mass media. In contrast, parents are often mainly concerned with maintaining their traditional family life and taking advantage of their new circumstances. As such, they tend to focus on the future and stress discipline and academic achievement for their children (Zhou 1997; Dublin 1996). There is some evidence, however, that the influence of authoritarian parenting, for example, is less negative for adolescent immigrants. Although second- and later-generation adolescents are likely to consider such parenting style un-American, immigrant adolescents are likely to perceive such parenting as natural (Dornbusch 1989; Dornbusch, Ritter, Leiderman, Roberts, and Fraleigh 1987).

Whereas there is much recognition of differences in acculturation with regards to parents and children, there is less recognition that variations in the acculturation of two parents within a home may also affect family process. Instances where a child shares an acculturative strategy with one parent, but not the other, may significantly strain relations between the child and the parent who feels excluded (Santisteban and Mitrani 2003). This may occur if child and mother, for example, feel that it is best to integrate with American society, but the father wishes to remain separate from the host culture and retain the identity of his original culture.

Gaps in the rate of acculturation between immigrant parents and children may also interact with contextual factors to affect adaptation outcomes. If children and their families reside in unfavorable contexts such as areas with poor labor market prospects and high levels of perceived discrimination, the likelihood of upward assimilation may be increased if parents and children experience the same rate of acculturation. In contrast, in the face of negative social context, a gap in the acculturation level of parents and children may significantly harm parent-child relationship and deny children access to family and community resources, thus allowing them to stray farther away from parental expectations (Zhou 1997; Portes and Rumbaut 1996). In such circumstances, immigrant children are likely to rebel and assimilate into an adverse context. This process is exemplified in West Indian children in New York City and Haitian children in Miami (Waters 1996; Waters 1994; Portes and Stepick 1993).

It is noteworthy that research has found that intergenerational conflicts within families do not necessarily mean negative adaptation outcomes (Schulz 1983). The ethnic community can often function as a mediator between an individual family and the larger society. Within tightly knit ethnic communities, immigrant parents and children are unlikely to keep their experiences to themselves. Instead, they are likely to share their experiences with other parents and children within the community. As these experiences tend to be similar across families, the community may act as a buffer that alleviates the tension between parents and their children (Zhou 1997).

SELECTION

An alternative explanation for the health and behavioral advantage frequently found among the foreign-born is selectivity (Landale et al. 1999; Hernandez and Charney 1998; Coll and Magnuson 1997). This perspective argues that the foreign-born may be healthier because individuals who are uncommonly healthy may be more likely to immigrate to the United States than those who are less healthy. Thus, rather than advantages of culture and social support, immigrants are self-selected from among the healthier population in their native countries and, after immigration, they simply retain relatively good health (Landale et al. 1999; Hernandez and Charney 1998). In addition to selection due to good health, immigrants could also be self-selected from among the highly educated, the more affluent, the highly motivated, and other segments that may provide them with an advantage upon immigrating to the U.S.

The argument with regard to selection has highlighted the importance of pre-migratory circumstances in the adjustment of immigrants (Portes and Rumbaut 1996). The characteristics of the country of origin and the immigrants' reasons for leaving may determine the health status of immigrants upon arrival in the U.S. and their later adjustment. For example, Portes and Rumbaut (1996) report that context of exit accounts for a large proportion of the differences in depression between refugees and other immigrants, with refugees experiencing greater depression.

Some researchers have argued that the issue of selection may be less salient for immigrant children. This argument is based on the notion that immigrant children are not self-selecting out of a population since they do not generally make the decision to migrate (Landale et al. 1999; Ashworth 1982). Adult family members generally make such decisions with little or no input from children. The counter argument, however, can be made that children may be affected because much research has shown that child outcomes are influenced by parental background and characteristics such as education, income, and well-being (Duncan, Yeung, Brooks-Gunn and Smith 1997). If adults who decide to migrate are more advantaged with regard to health and socioeconomic status, their children are also likely to be advantaged. Any decline in children's health and achievements upon immigrating, therefore, may simply be a regression to the mean; that is, children behaving more normally (Gans 1999).

Despite the possible influences of selection on immigrant adaptation, few studies can properly control for it. This general lack of proper controls is mainly due to the limitations of the data. Few national databases collect the types of data needed by immigration researchers on country of origin and immigration status, and few have the sample size necessary for sound conclusions on more than a few countries (Hernandez and Charney 1998).

OVERVIEW

This study focuses on immigrant generational variations in the health and behavior of youth. As outlined in this chapter, research tends to find some health advantage for foreign-born youth relative to their native-born counterparts. Much of the findings relate to physical health, with findings on mental health and behavior problems more ambiguous. There are several possible explanations for declining health with time spent in the United States, for example, acculturative stress, segmented assimilation, and intergenerational conflict. The potential influence of family process and social support are emphasized because of the generally strong impact of family and peers on socialization. This study examines whether factors such as parent-child conflict, independence in decision-making, parent-child closeness, parental involvement, and social support help to explain the relationship between immigrant generation and health and behavioral outcomes among youth.

This study does not test classical assimilation or segmented assimilation theories because the sample consists entirely of adolescents. What this research does investigate are the paths that immigrant youth take towards adaptation. Findings that the health and behavior of foreign-born youth are better than that of native-born youth and that health and behavior further deteriorates in subsequent generations, for example, would not support classical assimilation arguments. The classical assimilation argument is that (1) the lower well-being of the first-generation improves with each subsequent generation; and (2) well-being improves with each subsequent generation because each new generation is more American than the last generation. Although findings of deteriorating well-being in subsequent generations would indicate that youth in these higher generations are more American, being more American in this case would mean that youth have lower well-being, which is counter to the classical assimilation argument. The deterioration in health and behavior across generations would indicate that immigrant youth are on a downward assimilation path, likely being propelled by the stresses of acculturation such as cultural incompatibilities, intergenerational conflicts, poverty, and the inability to achieve important goals.

Although findings of deteriorating well-being would not support classical assimilation arguments, they would not necessarily support the arguments of segmented assimilation either. Segmented assimilation basically argues that whether or not well-being improves across generations depends on the segment of society to which these generations are assimilating. If they live in bad neighborhoods and interact with delinquent peers, they are more likely to assimilate downward and well-being will decrease over time and generations. In contrast, if they live in good neighborhoods and interact with non-delinquent peers, they are likely to assimilate upwards. Segmented assimilation theory, however, cannot be properly tested in this study.

Findings that health and behavior are better among native-born than foreign-born youth would support arguments of classical assimilation that well-being improves as immigrants blend into American society. The improvement in subsequent generations would indicate that immigrant youth are on an upward path towards assimilation.

Another argument that is examined in this study is that variations in family process among different generations of immigrant youth may help to explain the assimilation path being followed, that of improved well-being or deteriorating well-being. The many changes that accompany the assimilation process are likely to influence family process.

CHAPTER 3

Data and Measures

The sample used for this study is the 1995 National Longitudinal Study of Adolescent Health (commonly known as Add Health).[1] Add Health, a school-based study of adolescents in grades 7 through 12, examined the health-related behaviors of adolescents in the context of family, peers, school, neighborhood, and community. The Add Health sample was obtained through a random sample of all high schools in the United States. A total of 80 eligible schools were selected. Eligible high schools had to include an 11th grade and have an enrollment of over 30 students. The sample of schools was stratified by region of the country, level of urbanicity, school type (public/private) and size, ethnic composition (proportion black, proportion white), and grade span (e.g., 9 to 12, 10 to 12). The probability of selection for each school was based on size; thus, schools with higher enrollments had a greater probability of selection. Over 70 percent of high schools that were originally sampled were recruited into the study. Those schools that refused to participate were replaced with other high schools within the same strata.

Each high school recruited into the study was asked to identify its "feeder" schools. Feeder schools are those that include seventh grade and send a portion of their graduates to the recruited high school. As most high schools have more than one feeder school, one particular feeder school was selected for each high school with probability proportional to the number of its graduates who attended the high school; for example, a feeder school whose graduates made up one-quarter of the freshmen at a recruited high school had a selection probability of .25. The objective was to have a pair of schools (one high school and one junior high/middle school) in each of the 80 communities. In some cases the "pair" was a single school because high schools that spanned grades 7 through 12 served as their own feeder school. The resulting sample is comprised of 132 discrete schools—80 high schools and 52 junior high and middle schools.

Each student in grades 7 to 12 who was present during the predesignated class period that the questionnaire was administered to their particular school was asked to participate. More than 90,000 students completed this in-school questionnaire. A sample of students was also asked to complete an in-home interview. This in-home sample consisted of a core sample as well as specially selected oversamples. The core sample was selected from school rosters. Seventh to 12th grade students in each school were stratified by grade and sex. Approximately 17 students were chosen randomly from each stratum resulting in about 200 students selected from each high school/middle school pair. A total of 12,105 students were interviewed to form the core sample. Adolescents were selected for oversamples based on their responses on the In-School Questionnaire. The oversampled adolescents include (1) blacks with well-educated parents—at least one parent had a college degree, (2) Chinese, (3) Cubans, (4) Puerto Ricans, (5) the physically disabled, and (6) sibling pairs (e.g., twins, half-siblings). Additionally, to facilitate research on social networks, all students, rather than just 200, from 16 selected schools also completed in-home interviews. A total of 20,745 adolescents (including core and oversamples) completed in-home interviews.

A parent of each adolescent respondent was also asked to complete a "parent" questionnaire. This questionnaire covered topics such as household income, education and employment, inheritable health conditions, health behaviors, and marriages and marriage-like relations. A total of 17,700 parents were interviewed.

Sample weights[2] are available in Add Health in order to compensate for differences in selection probabilities and survey nonresponse. Weights, however, are only available for 18,924 adolescents in the 1995 data set. Adolescents without valid weights are those (1) who were added in the field; (2) who were selected as part of a sibling pair, but both siblings were not interviewed; and (3) who were without a sample flag.[3]

Add Health is appropriate for this study because it is a nationally representative dataset that provides extensive information on immigrant generation status and ethnic background. Not only does Add Health allow researchers to differentiate first- and second-generation immigrants from others, it also allows for detailed analysis of specific Hispanic (e.g., Mexican, Puerto Rican) and Asian (e.g., Chinese, Filipino) groups. The possibilities this allow are especially noteworthy given Add Health's large sample size. Additionally, this dataset provides extensive information on a broad array of topics related to family dynamics, health, behavior problems, and neighborhoods that are the focus of this research.

MEASURES
Dependent Variables

Depressive symptoms. Adolescents were asked to indicate how often they experienced each of the following emotions in the past week: (1) unable to shake off the blues, (2) felt depressed, (3) felt lonely, (4) felt sad, (5) bothered by things that usually don't bother you, (6) trouble keeping your mind on what you were doing, (7) hard to get started doing things, (8) poor appetite, (9) felt you were just as good as other people, (10) felt hopeful about the future, (11) felt life had been a failure, (12) felt fearful, (13) were happy, (14) talked less than usual, (15) others were mean to you, (16) enjoyed life, (17) felt people disliked you, and (18) felt too tired to do things. These are basic core items from the Center for Epidemiologic Studies Depression scale (Ross and Mirowsky 1984; Radloff 1977). These items are measured on a 4-point scale where 0 represents "never or rarely", 1 represents "sometimes", 2 represents "a lot of the time", and 3 represents "most of the time or all of the time". To maintain consistency, items (9), (10), (13), and (16) are reverse coded so that higher numbers represent greater frequency of negative emotions. Descriptive statistics are outlined in Appendix A. A reliability test indicates a Cronbach's alpha of .86. Responses to seven or more of these items are averaged to produce an index of depressive symptoms.

Positive affect. Four of the core items in the CES-D scale are used to measure positive affect. An index made up of these items is considered a reliable measure of positive affect (Ross and Mirowsky 1984). Adolescents were asked how often they experienced each of the following over the past week: (1) felt hopeful about the future, (2) happy, (3) enjoyed life, (4) felt you were just as good as other people.

Responses range from never or rarely (0) to most or all of the time (3). A reliability test indicates a Cronbach's alpha of .71. Responses are averaged to create the scale. Responses to at least two or more items are averaged to create the scale. *Deviant behavior scale.* Six items are used to construct this scale. Respondents were asked to report the frequency with which they engaged in particular activities in the past 12 months. The activities of interest are (1) "paint graffiti or signs on someone else's property or in a public place", (2) "deliberately damage property that didn't belong to you", (3) "lie to parents or guardians about where you had been or whom you were with", (4) "take something from a store without paying for it", (5) "steal something worth less than $50", and (6) be "loud, rowdy, or unruly in a public place". These items are part of a larger battery of 15 delinquent behaviors. Response choices are 0 "never", 1 "1 or 2 times", 2 "3 or 4 times", and 3 "5 or more times". Responses to two or more of these items are averaged to form an index of deviant behavior. These scale items were selected as they represent nonviolent acts and factor analysis results indicate that they represent a common factor. A reliability test of this deviant behavior scale indicates a Cronbach's alpha of .76.

Physiological response to stress index. This is a scaled measure that is based on adolescent response to nine items inquiring about the frequency with which adolescents had experienced particular health problems in the past 12 months. The health problems are: (1) headaches, (2) feeling hot all over suddenly and for no reason, (3) upset stomach or stomach ache, (4) cold sweats, (5) feeling physically weak for no reason, (6) cough or sore throat, (7) painful or frequent urination, (8) dizziness, (9) chest pains, and (10) muscle or joint aches, pains or soreness. Response choices are 0 "never", 1 "just a few times", 2 "about once a week", 3 "almost every day", and 4 "every day". Responses to four or more items are averaged to produce an index. For the most part, the items that make up this index are symptoms of biological stress and correspond to the "flight or fight" syndrome. The symptoms are produced when epinephrine, norepinephrine, and natural cortisone or cortisol are released in the body in response to environmental threats (Cannon 1932). Although each symptom may be caused by other factors, there is high positive correlation between symptoms because of the stress response, especially for adolescents. This measure, therefore, represents the frequency and intensity of the physiological response to environmental threats or stimuli.

Factor analysis was used to verify that the symptoms used in the physiological response index share a common factor. Results from principal axis extraction were similar for both varimax and oblimin rotations. Although initial results indicated two factors, the eigenvalue of the second factor barely exceeded one. Upon closer examination, it was determined that the two factors were simply blocks of similar frequencies—symptoms with high frequency made up one factor and symptoms with less frequency made up the second factor. This is a classic bias of exploratory factor analysis (Nunnally 1978). As a result of these findings, it was determined that the two factors were not meaningfully distinct; thus, a single factor index of physiological response was maintained. A reliability test indicates a Cronbach's alpha of .72.

Absence from school due to illness. This measure is based on adolescent response to the question, "In the last month, how often did a health or emotional problem cause you to miss a day of school?" Valid responses are 0 "never", 1 "just a few times", 2 "about once a week", 3 "almost every day", and 4 "every day".

General health status. This is a self-reported measure of overall health. The measure is derived from a single question that asked "In general, how is your health?" Response choices are 1 "excellent", 2 "very good", 3 "good", 4 "fair", and 5 "poor". The response choices were recoded so that higher numbers represent better physical health and lower numbers represent poorer health—i.e., 1 "poor", 2 "fair", 3 "good", 4 "very good", and 5 "excellent". This is a valid and reliable measure of general physical well-being (Mossey and Shapiro 1982; Davies and Ware 1981). Self-reported or perceived health is not simply a measure of the absence of morbidity, but rather, reflects diseases that are acute, chronic, fatal, and nonfatal as well as more general experiences of headaches and feeling tired. Perceived health is correlated with more "objective" measures of health such as the assessments of physicians made after clinical exams (Idler and Kasl 1991; Kaplan 1987; Mossey and Shapiro 1982). Self-reported health is actually a stronger predictor of mortality than a physician's assessment (Mossey and Shapiro 1982) and predicts mortality "over and above" measures of disease, health behavior (e.g., smoking or exercise), and physical disability (Idler and Kasl 1991; Liang 1986; Davies and Ware 1981).

Independent Measures

<u>Individual Characteristics</u>

Immigrant generation status. This variable is measured by a set of dummy variables contrasting first-, second-, and third- and higher-generation immigrant youth. The definition used for this study is the same as that which is frequently used by researchers who study immigrant adaptation (e.g., Harker 2001; Harris 1999; Kao 1999; Hernandez and Charney 1998; Hogan and Eggebeen 1997). Adolescents who are foreign-born and who have at least one parent who is also foreign-born are coded as first-generation immigrants. Adolescents who are U.S.-born but who have at least one parent who is foreign-born are coded as second-generation immigrants. Of the youth who are coded second-generation, approximately one-half have only one parent who is foreign-born and the other one-half have two parents who are foreign-born. The third- and higher-generation group consists of cases where both adolescents and their parents are U.S.-born. There are instances where adolescents are American citizens at birth despite being born in a foreign country. These circumstances may occur if American parents, whether born or legalized, are working or vacationing abroad at the time of their child's birth. Adolescents who report such circumstances are coded as second-generation if at least one parent is foreign-born and are coded as third- and higher-generation if their parents are U.S.-born. Generation status for 221 U.S.-born adolescents could not be determined due to the lack of information on their parents' origin. Discriminant analysis was used to classify these missing cases into one of two groups—second-generation or third- and higher-generation. The cases were not first-generation as they were U.S.-born.[4]

Age at arrival. This variable measures the age at which first-generation adolescent immigrants moved to the United States for the first time. This measure is important given that time and the changes that occur with it are central to explanations for immigrant adaptation outcomes. Age at arrival is an indicator of time in the country as well as an indicator of developmental stage at the time of arrival and is related to adaptation (Rumbaut 1994a; Cropley 1983). As this measure is only applicable to adolescents coded as first-generation immigrants, it is an internal or conditionally relevant variable. To test the hypotheses that the effect of first-generation immigrant status depends on the age at arrival in the U.S. it is necessary that the models represent the differences in dependent measures between adolescents who are first-, second-, and third- and higher-generation, as well as show how such differences vary depending on age at arrival. The three immigrant generations, therefore, will be compared while simultaneously representing the effect of age at arrival, a variable that is only applicable to first-generation adolescents. The required model is illustrated in Equation 1 (Ross and Mirowsky 1992; Cohen 1968).

$$\ln(D) = b_0 + [b_1 + b_2(A - \overline{A}_F)]F + u \qquad (1)$$

$$\ln(D) = b_0 + b_1 F + b_2[(A - \overline{A}_F)F] + u \qquad (2)$$

D represents the dependent variable, A represents age at arrival and is measured in deviations from the mean for foreign-born adolescents, and F is the dummy variable representing whether the adolescent is foreign-born or U.S.-born. The expression in the square brackets in Equation 1 represents the change in the dependent measure that is associated with foreign birth. The model is estimated through the process of multiplying the square bracket in equation 1 by the foreign-born dummy variable and entering the b_2 portion of the equation as an independent variable controlling for F (Equation 2).

Language. Adolescents were asked to report what language is usually spoken in their home. Language is measured as a dummy variable contrasting those adolescents who report that English is usually spoken at home and those who report that another language is most frequently spoken. Language is included as a control measure as language difficulties may contribute to acculturative stress and intergenerational conflict (Hernandez and Charney 1998).

Ethnic background. This variable is measured by three sets of dummy variables: Hispanic background, Asian background, and other backgrounds. In the Add Health questionnaire, adolescents who identified themselves as Hispanics or Asians were asked to more specifically define their ethnic background. The Hispanic background set of dummy variables contrasts four backgrounds: Mexican/Chicano, Cuban, Puerto Rican, and Other Hispanic. Puerto Ricans born in Puerto Rico (the mainland) are considered immigrants for purposes of this study since their experiences are likely similar to those of other immigrant groups (Harris 1999). The dummy variables for Asian background contrast Chinese, Filipino, and Other Asian backgrounds. These variables are included to more clearly identify differences within Hispanic and Asian groups, differences that have been recognized but that are usually not examined because of inadequate sample sizes. Adolescents of other backgrounds are represented by dummy variables for African/Black and European/White backgrounds. Although each of the latter two groups represent individuals from a large diversity of countries that may be represented differently across immigrant generations, the groups are combined here simply for comparison purposes. Small sample sizes for first-generation respondents prevented ethnic breakdowns within these two larger groups. The ethnic backgrounds of individuals who were classified other minorities were determined from country of birth data.

Other characteristics. Age is measured in years with a mean of 15.5. Sex is coded 1 for females and 0 for males. Forty-nine percent of the sample is female.

Family and Parent Characteristics
Several family and parent characteristics are used as control measures. It is well-known that characteristics such as family structure, household size, and socioeconomic status are related to the health and behavior of adolescents (e.g., McLeod and Sandefur 1996; McLanahan and Sandefur 1994; Gore, Aseltine and Colten 1992; Baydar 1988). Descriptive statistics for these variables are outlined in Appendix A.

Family structure. Family structure is indicated by a set of dummy variables contrasting two-parent, step-parent, one-parent, and other households. Two-parent households include two biological or adoptive parents. Step-parent households consist of remarried individuals as well as cohabiting couples. One-parent households consist of parents living without partners in the household. Other households are those of other family structures such as those headed by grandparents and other adults. Family structure is believed to affect well-being by influencing family functioning (Sandefur and Mosley 1997); for example, research has found that parental supervision and involvement are lower in single-parent than two-parent families (McLanahan 1988) and that children in single-parent families are more likely to engage in delinquent acts (McLanahan and Booth 1989).

Extended households. A measure of extended households is represented by a dummy variable that contrasts homes with adults other than parents or siblings and those without. Examples of adults other than parents and siblings who may be residing in the household include grandparents, aunts, uncles, and other related or unrelated adults. This extended household measure is included because such households may be more frequent in first-generation immigrant families (Perez 1996), especially during early years in the United States. Thus, such households may influence adolescent outcomes during these years. The influence may be positive in that they provide emotional and financial support, but it may also be negative in that they reinforce the culture of their homeland and lead to more conflict between children who want to fit into American society and their parents.

Household size. Household size represents the total number of individuals residing in the home including the adolescent respondent. This variable is included as a control measure because immigrants living in large households may have different experiences than those in small households. Immigrant youth in large households, for example, will likely have to share resources more than youth with smaller households. An example of an important resource is parents' time and attention. Insufficient attention and time may affect adolescent health and behavior. Additionally, research on sibling size (Blake 1981) and interactions in small groups (Hogan and Eggebeen 1997) suggest a link between household size and adolescent well-being with adolescents in smaller size households exhibiting better well-being, especially with regard to educational achievement.

Household income. Income is obtained from parent response to a question that asks: "About how much total income, before taxes did your family receive in 1994? Include your own income, the income of everyone else in your household, and income from welfare benefits, dividends, and all other sources." Responses are coded in units of 1000. As there are a large number of missing cases associated with parent response in the Add Health data, household income is imputed for the approximately 26 percent of cases missing this variable or who reported zero income. Those with zero income are included in the sample with imputed values because reports of zero household income, as opposed to individual income, appear suspicious and are recoded to missing. Predicted values from a regression equation on valid cases are used to impute values for missing cases. A dummy variable is subsequently included to represent whether values are predicted (1) or not predicted (0). With this procedure, it is possible to test for and correct any biases resulting from the inclusion of predicted values (Cohen and Cohen 1983). Both household income and parents' education, discussed below, are included to control for socioeconomic status, which is often linked to adolescent health and behavior.

Parents' education. This is a measure of the highest level of education completed. It is based on both parent and adolescent responses. Adolescent responses are only used if parent responses are missing. If the education levels of two parents are provided, the education level that is highest is used. Education is imputed for the 1.8 percent of cases with missing values.

Family Process and Social Support Measures

As outlined in the previous chapter, there is much evidence that family factors are associated with the well-being of children and adolescents (e.g., Patten et al. 1997; Rumbaut 1994a; Dornbusch 1989; Marjoribanks 1987; Steinberg 1986). Additionally, there is evidence that individuals who perceive high levels of social support from parents, friends, and other adults report better health (e.g., Wickrama, Lorenz, and Conger 1997; Patten et al. 1997; Zhou 1997; Short and Johnston 1997; Thoits 1995). In instances of missing values, the independent variables outlined above are used to impute values on the family process measures outlined below.

Independence in decision-making. This variable is a 7-item index that measures the extent to which adolescents are allowed to make their own decisions and rules. Adolescents were asked "do your parents let you make your own decisions about": (1) the time you must be home on weekend nights, (2) the people you hang around with, (3) what you wear, (4) how much television you watch, (5) which television programs you watch, (6) what time you go to bed on weeknights, and (7) what you eat. Response choices are "yes" or "no". A reliability test indicates a Cronbach's alpha of .63. Responses to three or more of these items are averaged to produce an index. Values are imputed for the 2.1 percent of cases that had missing values on this index.

Parental expectations for education. This index is created from two items asked separately about mother's and father's expectations. Respondents were asked how disappointed each of their parents would be if they failed to graduate from (1) college, and (2) high school. Responses range from 1 (low disappointment) to 5 (high disappointment). The reliability coefficient for the four items is .81. Responses are averaged to create an index. Values for the 2.4 percent of cases that are missing on this index are imputed.

Parental involvement. This index is composed of nine items that inquire into the activities that parents and adolescents do together within a 4-week period. Adolescents were asked if they had done each of the following with each parent: (1) gone shopping, (2) played a sport, (3) attended a religious service or related event, (4) talked about a date or party attended, (5) attended a movie, sports event, concert, play, or museum, (6) talked about a personal problem, (7) discussed grades or school work, (8) worked on a school project, and (9) talked about other school activities. Response choices are "yes" and "no". The activities in which the adolescent and at least one parent had engaged are summed to form the index. The scale has a Cronbach's alpha of .56. Values are imputed for the 3.6 percent of cases missing on this index.

Parent-child conflict. Adolescents were asked how often they had a serious argument with their parents. Adolescents who argued with at least one of their parents during the 4-week period prior to the survey are coded 1 for having experienced parent-child conflict. Those who did not argue with a parent during this time are coded 0. Discriminant analysis is used to estimate whether or not conflict occurred in the 2.2 percent of cases who did not respond to this question.[5]

Parent-child closeness. Adolescent responses to four items asked about each parent separately are used to construct this index. The items are (1) how close do you feel to your mother/father, (2) how much do you feel that he/she cares about you, (3) he/she is warm and loving towards you most of the time, and (4) overall, you are satisfied with your relationship with your mother/father. Responses to items (1) and (2) range from 1 (not at all) to 5 (very much). Responses to items (3) and (4) range from 1 (strongly agree) to 5 (strongly disagree), but are reverse coded in order to match the response scale for the first two items. High scores indicate positive or good parent-child relationships. Valid responses to three or more of these items are used to construct an index. This scale has a Cronbach's alpha of .84. Values are imputed for 2.1 percent of cases.

Social support. Eight items are used to construct this scale. Adolescents were asked how much they feel that: (1) adults care about them, (2) teachers care about them, (3) parents care about them, (4) friends care about them, (5) people in the family understand them, (6) they want to leave home, (7) their family have fun together, and (8) their family pays attention to them. Items are measured on a 5-point scale ranging from 1 (not at all) to 5 (very much). The response to the item that asked the extent to which adolescents want to leave home is reverse coded to make it compatible with the other items such that higher numbers represent stronger feelings that others care for them. Responses to three or more of these items are averaged to produce an index. A reliability test indicates a Cronbach's alpha of .78. Factor analysis results indicate that these items represent a common factor.

Values are imputed for the 0.5 percent of cases with missing values on this index.

Contextual Variables

Given increasing awareness of the potential influence of community or neighborhood characteristics on adolescent outcomes (Portes and Zhou 1993), several contextual variables are included in the analyses: region of residence, urban/rural location, and the proportion of the neighborhood in poverty, foreign-born, and the same race as the respondent. These are commonly used measures in studies of immigrant population. The high concentration of immigrants in the Western portion of the country and in large cities (Lollock 2001; Rumbaut 1994b) makes it important to control for region. Research has shown that adolescents in poor neighborhoods experience greater health and behavioral problems (Aneshensel and Sucoff 1996). Additionally, the proportion foreign-born is an indicator of the immigrant/non-immigrant composition of the neighborhood, which may influence support networks and adherence to cultural values.

Two contextual variables were obtained from the questionnaire completed by the administrator of each sampled school: region of the country and location of residence. *Region* is a four category dummy variable representing Northeast, Midwest, South, and West. *Location* is a three category dummy variable representing urban, suburban, and rural areas. The remaining three contextual variables were obtained from Add Health's contextual database in which geocodes were used to link respondent home addresses to various Census areas, namely state, county, tract, and block group. *Proportion of persons with income below the poverty line* and *proportion of foreign-born persons* were taken directly from the contextual database. Variables that measured the proportion of persons of each race were used to create a variable that measured the *proportion of persons of the same race as the respondent*. This variable is more useful for this study because it indicates the extent to which the community and the individual are similar with regard to race, rather than simply measuring proportion white or proportion black without considering the race of the respondent. The latter three variables are based on data from the Summary Tape File 3A (STF 3A) of the 1990 Census of Population and Housing (Billy, Wenzlow, and Grady 1998). Census tract level data are used for these variables. Although block level data are more frequently used and may be more accurate in many instances, census tract data may be more relevant for adolescents. Adolescents are likely to have friends from a wider area than a block group because high schools draw students from a wider area and thus adolescents are more likely to be influenced by that larger area.

In a small proportion of cases (one percent or less), contextual data are missing due to unavailable geocodes or unstable estimates as a result of small sample sizes. Geocodes were deemed unavailable in cases where (1) respondent addresses could not be accurately matched to a particular state, country, tract or block group, or (2) the address could only be associated with zip code information that cannot accurately identify smaller areas such as tract and block group (Billy et al. 1998). Missing data due to unstable estimates resulted when there were concerns that the sample data on which the estimates of community characteristics are based may not reflect the actual population values. The smaller the sample on which the estimates are based, the lower the confidence in their accuracy. Estimates from the STF 3A Census data are based on sample data because they are derived from the Census long form that was only administered to one of every six or seven households (Billy et al. 1998). As the missing and non-missing cases do not differ on the dependent variables, the means are substituted for missing values on proportion in poverty, proportion foreign-born, and proportion same race, and a dummy variable is created to control for whether the values are predicted or not predicted.

ANALYSIS

The complexity of Add Health's design structure necessitates the use of survey software that can properly incorporate the characteristics of the survey design in its statistical computations. As clusters were sampled with unequal probability, observations are not independent and identically distributed. The statistical package must be able to account for the clustering and correlation of the data in order to produce unbiased estimates of variances and standard errors. Obtaining such unbiased results through the use of traditional statistical packages such as SPSS and SAS is time consuming and difficult. STATA is used for analyses in this study because it is a survey software package that is capable of computing unbiased variances, standard errors, and point estimates such as means and regression parameters efficiently. Adjustments are made for the design structure of the dataset in STATA by specifying the cluster variable, the stratification variable, and the design type. The primary sampling unit or cluster variable is the school from which the adolescent was sampled. The stratification variable is the region (Northeast, Midwest, South, and West) of the country. Although a stratification variable was not included in Add Health's sampling plan, a post-stratification adjustment was made to the sample weights to allow the use of region for this purpose. This involved making an adjustment to the initial school weights for each region so that the sum of the school weights equaled the total number of schools on the sampling frame for each region. The design type is "with replacement" sampling. Designers assumed this design type although schools were not returned to the sample pool (or placed back on the sample list) before the next school was selected. Add Health designers use the fact that the variance estimation technique was obtained using large sample theory to justify this assumption (Chantala and Tabor 1999).

Much of the analysis is based on weighted data in order to account for unequal probability of selection and survey nonresponse. The 1,821 cases without valid weights are excluded from the analyses so that the unweighted and weighted tabulations will be based on the same observations or cases (Chantala and Tabor 1999).

Transformations
Most of the dependent variables in the analyses are highly skewed. This is not surprising given the outcome variables and the age group being studied. Skewed variables can produce heteroscedasticity and inflated standard errors of the estimates in regression analysis. These problems reduce the statistical power of significance tests, which result in larger confidence intervals and make the rejection of the null hypotheses more difficult (Hamilton 1992; Berk 1983). The potential loss of statistical power is especially important when testing multiple product terms (Hamilton 1992). In order to increase the power of the significance tests, self-rated health, physiological stress response, depression, and deviant behavior are transformed. This is accomplished by means of calculating the square root of each and using the transformed variables in regression analyses. The square root variant was chosen after testing the effects of several alternatives on the skewness of the variables. The raw score, the cube transformation, and the square-root transformation were compared, and, if the variable had a zero value, it was transformed by recoding values of zero to one-half of the lowest possible score. This latter recode is imposing a value other than zero because it is highly unlikely that respondents

experienced no symptoms. For each variable the square root transformation most effectively reduced the skewness. The measure of positive affect is not transformed because the raw score is less skewed than the alternatives.

In addition to transforming some of the dependent variables, several independent variables were also transformed. Continuous independent variables used in interaction terms are centered. This involves subtracting each value by the individual variable mean. Centering reduces the risk of multicollinearity, generates a constant that is interpretable, and helps in the interpretation of interactions (Aiken and West 1991). Logged transformations of household income are also used to reduce the disproportionate effect that changes can have across the range of values for these variables.

Stages of analysis
The first part of the analysis is descriptive. Correlations of immigrant generation and family process with predictor and control variables are outlined in Appendix A.2. Separate variable means for first-, second-, and third- and higher-generations are outlined in Appendix A.3. Separate variable means are also provided for each immigrant generation within each of the nine ethnic groups of interest in Appendix A.4. The remaining analyses were conducted using multiple regression techniques. Each chapter includes a detailed outline of the analytic strategy used to address the research question.

CHAPTER 4

Health and Behavior

This chapter examines the association between adolescent immigrant generation status and health and behavioral outcomes. This is the first step in addressing the larger research question of whether family process can help to explain any association between immigrant generation status and adolescents' health and behavior. Although previous research has examined the relationship between immigrant generation and health and behavioral outcomes, it is important to establish the nature of the association with the outcome measures in this study before proceeding to the larger research question.

In examining the research question of whether there is an association between immigrant generation and health and behavioral outcomes, this study will address one of the main issues in migration research on adolescents: Do foreign-born youth report better health and behavior than youth born in the United States? It could be assumed that the foreign-born are in worse health given that families tend to migrate in order to improve their economic and/or social circumstances and that the migration process is likely to invoke a significant amount of stress. Theories of adult immigrant adaptation do not provide a consistent answer. Based on the classical assimilation perspective, native-born youth should exhibit better health and behavior since they engage in a lifestyle that the foreign-born strive for and can only achieve through the assimilation process. The assumption is that the change in circumstances induced by the assimilation process is always positive. In contrast to the classical perspective, the segmented assimilation perspective would be that whether foreign-born youth

47

report better or worse health and behavior depends on the segment of society to which these youth are assimilating. If they are residing in high crime communities, for example, then they will likely exhibit health and behavioral outcomes similar to those of the population in that community. Research studies that have addressed the issue of whether or not the foreign-born exhibit better health and behavior have also been somewhat inconsistent. The majority of findings, however, seem to indicate more positive health and behavior among foreign-born than native-born youth (Harris 1999; Hernandez and Charney 1998). There are even findings that among the native-born population, those with foreign-born parents report better health and behavior than those with native-born parents (e.g., Harker 2001; Harris 1999).

Given the findings of other researchers and the arguments proposed to address the issue of immigrant generation and health and behavioral outcomes, results may indicate that foreign-born youth have better health and behavior than native-born youth. On the other hand, results may indicate that they have worse health and behavior than native-born youth. Thus, both hypotheses are tested.

As the assimilation process is not likely to be complete before the third-generation, native-born youth with foreign-born parents may differ significantly from those with native-born parents. Native-born youth with foreign-born parents, thus, may have better or worse health and behavior than native-born youth with native-born parents.

ANALYTIC STRATEGY

Two methods of statistical analysis are used for analysis: ordinary least squares regression and ordered logit. Ordinary least squares regression is used to test the association between immigrant generation and depressive symptoms, positive affect, deviant behavior, physiological response to stressors, and overall health. Ordered logit is used to test the association between immigrant generation and absence from school due to illness in order to better represent the ordered nature of the scale used to measure school absences.

The results of the regression analyses are outlined in Tables 4.1 through 4.6. The tables include unstandardized coefficients with standard errors in brackets. Equation 1 of each table presents the bivariate association between generation and health and behavioral outcomes. Equation 2 adjusts for sociodemographic and community factors. Standard controls are included for age and sex as well as controls for family and parent characteristics, community context, language use, and age at arrival. Separate analyses were conducted with time in the U.S. substituted for age at arrival; however, this substitution had no significant effect on results. Age at arrival is used throughout the remaining analyses. Equation 3 includes further controls for ethnic background. Ethnic background is included separately to better sort through the factors that influence the association between immigrant generation and each outcome. The effect of ethnicity can be identified after controlling for other sociodemographic factors. Additionally, it can be determined how adjusting for ethnicity affects the association between immigrant generation and health and the association between community factors and health.

The tables outline differences in health and behavioral outcomes between foreign-born youth (first-generation) and native-born youth with native-born parents (third- and higher-generation, the reference category) as well as differences between native-born youth with foreign-born parents (second-generation) and native-born youth with native-born parents (third- and higher-generation). Differences between first- and second-generation youth are only presented in the text.

RESULTS
Do foreign-born youth have better or worse health and behavior compared to youth of other generations? These results do not provide a consistent answer across outcomes. First-generation youth report less deviant behavior and less physiological stress response than youth of other generations and these generational differences are not due to sociodemographic or community factors. In contrast, first-generation youth have higher levels of depressive symptoms and lower positive affect than youth of other generations, but these generational differences are due to sociodemographic factors, particularly household income, parental education, and household size. Results for school absence due to illness and overall health are more complex. The findings that first-generation youth have fewer school absences due to illness and are in better overall health are only attained after controlling for sociodemographic and community characteristics.

An important component of examining multiple generations of immigrants is the question of whether there are important differences among native-born youth. Do health and behavioral outcomes of native-born youth differ between those youth with foreign-born parents and those with native-born parents? Although second-generation youth

Table 4.1. Depressive Symptoms[a] Regressed on Immigrant Generation

	Equation 1	Equation 2	Equation 3
1st generation[b]	.062 (.016)***	-.014 (.016)	-.025 (.016)
2nd generation[b]	.027 (.013)*	.002 (.010)	-.003 (.011)
Generation pred	.100 (.028)***	-.031 (.035)	-.030 (.035)
Age[c]		.016 (.002)***	.016 (.002)***
Age at arrival[d]		.003 (.002)	.003 (.002)
Female		.057 (.006)***	.058 (.006)***
Family structure[e]			
Step-parent		.045 (.008)***	.046 (.008)***
One-parent		.048 (.008)***	.048 (.008)***
Other		.061 (.013)***	.061 (.013)***
English in home		-.004 (.018)	-.010 (.017)
Extended family		.006 (.009)	.006 (.009)
Household size		.013 (.002)***	.013 (.002)***
Household income[c]		-.015 (.005)**	-.016 (.005)**
Parents' education[c]		-.009 (.001)***	-.009 (.001)***
Education predicted		.060 (.025)*	.060 (.025)*
Region[f]			
Midwest		-.011 (.014)	-.006 (.014)
South		-.017 (.014)	-.011 (.014)
Northeast		-.007 (.014)	-.011 (.014)
Residence[g]			
Suburb		.015 (.009)†	.013 (.009)
Rural		.006 (.012)	.005 (.012)
Prop. same ethnicity		-.031 (.011)**	-.025 (.014)†
Prop. foreign-born		.034 (.052)	.063 (.044)
Prop. poor		.081 (.025)**	.078 (.029)**
Ethnicity[h]			
Mexican			.002 (.013)
Cuban			-.077 (.036)*
Puerto Rican			.028 (.019)
Other Hispanic			-.027 (.020)
Chinese			.018 (.032)
Filipino			.065 (.024)**
Other Asian			.019 (.021)
African/Black			.002 (.012)
Constant	.719	.631	.628
R^2	.005	.070	.072

*** p<.001, ** p<.01, * p<.05, † p<.10 (two-tailed test)
[a]The square root of this variable is used to adjust for skewness. [b]Reference category is third and later generations. [c]Measured as mean deviation. [d]Conditionally relevant variable. For first generation immigrant youth, these variables test whether the effect of being foreign-born depends on the age at arrival. [e]Reference category is two-parent households. [f]Reference category is west. [g]Reference category is urban. [h]Reference category is European/White.

are advantaged with less physiological stress response and disadvantaged with greater depressive symptoms, lower positive affect, and greater deviant behavior compared to third- and higher-generation youth, all of these differences are explained by sociodemographic and community factors. Second-generation and third- and higher-generation youth have similar school absences due to illness and overall health regardless of whether sociodemographic and community characteristics are controlled. Second-generation and third- and higher-generation youth, therefore, are generally similar in their health and behavior.

Results also indicate that several variables that were expected to have large and significant associations with health and behavioral outcomes are actually of much less importance. Such variables include age at arrival in the U.S. and language usually spoken in the home. These will be discussed in a subsequent section of this chapter.

Depressive Symptoms
Depressive symptoms and depression are used interchangeably in the presentation of study findings in this chapter as well as in remaining chapters. The measure used, however, represents an index of depressive symptoms, not a diagnosis of depression.

As indicated earlier, first-generation youth appear to be significantly more depressed than second-generation youth $[F(1,128)=7.97, p<.01]$ and third- and higher-generation youth (Table 4.1). Second-generation youth are also more depressed than third- and higher-generation youth. Although there are fewer depressive symptoms on average among second-generation youth, a significant overlap in the 95 percent confidence intervals for first- and second-generation youth indicates that the difference in means may be small.

Although the bivariate results indicate significant differences in depressive symptoms between immigrant generations, adjusting for sociodemographic and community factors reduce the differences between immigrant generations to nonsignificance. Sociodemographic and community factors, thus, seem to account for the positive association between immigrant generation and depressive symptoms.

Further examination of the control variables indicates that greater depressive symptoms among first-generation youth is due mainly to their lower household income and parental education, and higher household size and age relative to youth of other generations. Greater depressive symptoms among second-generation relative to third- and higher-generation youth is also due to these factors. Table

Table 4.2. Positive Affect Regressed on Immigrant Generation

	Equation 1	Equation 2	Equation 3
1st generation[a]	-.202 (.039)***	.006 (.044)	.039 (.046)
2nd generation[a]	-.115 (.030)***	-.030 (.024)	-.010 (.027)
Generation pred	-.129 (.057)*	.112 (.081)	.108 (.081)
Age[b]		-.010 (.004)*	-.010 (.004)*
Age at arrival[c]		-.008 (.005)	-.009 (.006)
Female		-.064 (.014)***	-.065 (.014)***
Family structure[d]			
Step-parent		-.075 (.018)***	-.078 (.018)***
One-parent		-.046 (.023)†	-.047 (.023)*
Other		-.095 (.039*	-.096 (.039)*
English in home		.050 (.047)	.049 (.046)
Extended family		-.006 (.024)	-.006 (.024)
Household size		-.025 (.005)***	-.023 (.005)***
Household income[b]		.038 (.014)**	.040 (.014)**
Parents' education[b]		.029 (.003)***	.029 (.003)***
Education predicted		-.146 (.067)*	-.143 (.066)*
Region[e]			
Midwest		.027 (.035)	.010 (.033)
South		.029 (.034)	.007 (.032)
Northeast		-.015 (.036)	-.035 (.034)
Residence[f]			
Suburb		-.042 (.022)†	-.039 (.022)†
Rural		-.031 (.032)	-.030 (.031)
Prop. same ethnicity		.040 (.025)	.006 (.029)
Prop. foreign-born		-.134 (.121)	-.187 (.104)†
Prop. poor		-.196 (.069)**	-.190 (.074)*
Ethnicity[g]			
Mexican			-.078 (.039)*
Cuban			.138 (.060)*
Puerto Rican			-.027 (.051)
Other Hispanic			.056 (.054)
Chinese			-.033 (.068)
Filipino			-.193 (.078)*
Other Asian			-.104 (.059)†
African/Black			-.011 (.028)
Constant	2.041	2.168	2.212
R^2	.007	.050	.052

*** p<.001, ** p<.01, * p<.05, † p<.10 (two-tailed test)
[a]Reference category is third and later generations. [b]Measured as mean deviation. [c]Conditionally relevant variable. For first generation immigrant youth, these variables test whether the effect of being foreign-born depends on the age at arrival. [d]Reference category is two-parent households. [e]Reference category is west. [f]Reference category is urban. [g]Reference category is European/White.

4.1 also indicates that youth who are female, older than average, do not reside in two-parent households, live in larger size households, have lower household income and parental education, and live in high poverty neighborhoods report more depressive symptoms than other youth. In addition, Filipinos report more depressive symptoms, and Cubans report less, than youth of European background.

Overall, hypotheses of greater depressive symptoms among first- and second-generation youth are supported, but only at the bivariate level. This finding of no significant differences in levels of depressive symptoms across immigrant generations net of sociodemographic and community factors is not that unusual given the low consistency of research findings that relate to immigrant generation and mental health relative to physical health. Although some studies appear to find less depressive symptoms among the first-generation, the findings in this study add to the inconsistency in the mental health literature where there are some findings of no effect after controlling for demographic and community factors like age, sex, socioeconomic status, and region of the country (Portes and Rumbaut 1996; Malzberg and Lee 1956), findings of lower emotional distress (Harker 2001; Harris 1999), and other findings of higher emotional problems (Kao 1999).

Positive Affect
The results for positive affect (Table 4.2) are very similar to those just outlined for depression. Both first- and second-generation youth have significantly lower levels of positive affect than third- and higher-generation youth at the bivariate level. Additionally, first-generation youth also have lower positive affect than second-generation youth [$F(1,128)=6.24$, $p<.05$]. As with depression, however, adjusting for sociodemographic and community characteristics reduces the association to nonsignificance and further controls for ethnic background have no effect.

Examinations of the association between the control variables and positive affect and the association between the control variables and immigrant generation status indicate that the higher positive affect among first- and second-generation youth is largely explained by less parental education, lower household income, and greater household size relative to third- and higher-generation youth. The other sociodemographic variables have less explanatory influence. This is similar to findings for depression, except that age had a greater influence on explaining depression.

Table 4.3. Deviant Behavior[a] Regressed on Immigrant Generation

	Equation 1	Equation 2	Equation 3
1st generation[b]	-.087 (.021)***	-.101 (.029)**	-.117 (.028)***
2nd generation[b]	.043 (.018)*	.025 (.019)	.012 (.020)
Age[c]		.005 (.003)	.006 (.003)†
Age at arrival[d]		-.017 (.003)***	-.016 (.003)***
Female		-.043 (.008)***	-.043 (.008)***
Family structure[e]			
Step-parent		.052 (.012)***	.053 (.012)***
One-parent		.054 (.012)***	.060 (.012)***
Other		.029 (.020)	.037 (.020)†
English in home		.024 (.026)	.042 (.026)
Extended family		-.007 (.014)	-.007 (.014)
Household size		.002 (.003)	.003 (.003)
Household income[c]		.011 (.009)	.009 (.009)
Parents' education[c]		.004 (.002)*	.005 (.002)**
Region[f]			
Midwest		.013 (.025)	.019 (.026)
South		-.050 (.023)*	-.040 (.025)
Northeast		.012 (.030)	.021 (.029)
Residence[g]			
Suburb		-.014 (.015)	-.012 (.015)
Rural		-.036 (.024)	-.037 (.025)
Prop. same ethnicity		-.054 (.017)**	-.056 (.023)*
Prop. foreign-born		.123 (.058)*	.103 (.072)
Prop. poor		-.207 (.061)**	-.160 (.062)*
Ethnicity[h]			
Mexican			.041 (.025)
Cuban			.019 (.050)
Puerto Rican			.027 (.034)
Other Hispanic			.021 (.031)
Chinese			-.017 (.044)
Filipino			.045 (.038)
Other Asian			.046 (.038)
African/Black			-.047 (.017)**
Constant	.516	.582	.552
R^2	.004	.029	.031

*** $p<.001$, ** $p<.01$, * $p<.05$, † $p<.10$ (two-tailed test)
[a]The square root of this variable is used to adjust for skewness. [b]Reference category is third and later generations. [c]Measured as mean deviation. [d]Conditionally relevant variable. For first generation immigrant youth, these variables test whether the effect of being foreign-born depends on the age at arrival. [e]Reference category is two-parent households. [f]Reference category is west. [g]Reference category is urban. [h]Reference category is European/White.

An examination of the confidence intervals for positive affect indicates an overlap for first- and second-generation youth. A distinctly different level of positive affect, however, is evident among third- and higher-generation youth, a pattern that is similar to that for depression. Table 4.2 indicates that youth with low positive affect and high depression share many of the same characteristics.

These findings, like those for depressive symptoms, support the hypotheses of worse health among youth in lower immigrant generations, but only at the bivariate level. Differences in positive affect across generations are largely explained by parental education and household income and size.

Behavior
In contrast to findings of diminished emotional well-being among first-generation youth with regard to depression and positive affect, results for deviant behavior indicate less deviance among first-generation youth than among second-generation [F(1,128)=31.37, p<.001] and third- and higher-generation youth (Table 4.3). An examination of the confidence intervals highlights the large differences in average deviant behavior across immigrant generations with second-generation youth experiencing the most deviant behavior. These differences between immigrant generations persist, and are actually strengthened, after controlling for sociodemographic and community factors.

Surprisingly, differences in deviant behavior between second-generation and third- and higher-generation youth indicate more, rather than less, deviance among second-generation youth. Although this finding reflects the disadvantage of second-generation youth relative to third- and higher-generation youth evident for depression and positive affect, it undermines the idea that behavior would consistently increase or decrease across higher immigrant generations as it has for previously discussed outcomes. The difference between second-generation and third- and higher-generation youth, however, is reduced to nonsignificance after controlling for sociodemographic and community factors.

Controlling for ethnic background reduces some community variables to nonsignificance. The greater deviant behavior experienced by youth living in communities with larger proportions of foreign-born persons, and the less deviant behavior of those living in the South relative to the West, are explained by ethnic background. There is also evidence that foreign-born youth who immigrate at an

Table 4.4. Physiological Stress Response[a] Regressed on Immigrant Generation

	Equation 1	Equation 2	Equation 3
1st generation[b]	-.075 (.016)***	-.047 (.017)**	-.055 (.016)**
2nd generation[b]	-.032 (.009)**	-.015 (.009)	-.018 (.009)†
Age[c]		-.202E-3 (.002)	.315E-3 (.002)
Age at arrival[d]		-.003 (.002)	-.003 (.002)
Female		.062 (.005)***	.063 (.005)***
Family structure[e]			
Step-parent		.021 (.006)***	.021 (.006)***
One-parent		.019 (.007)*	.024 (.007)**
Other		.014 (.012)	.020 (.012)†
English in home		.011 (.013)	.011 (.013)
Extended family		.010 (.008)	.009 (.007)
Household size		.004 (.002)*	.005 (.002)**
Household income[c]		.006 (.005)	.004 (.005)
Parents' education[c]		.001 (.001)	.001 (.001)
Region[f]			
Midwest		-.005 (.014)	-.002 (.014)
South		-.010 (.014)	-.004 (.014)
Northeast		-.030 (.017)†	-.029 (.017)†
Residence[g]			
Suburb		-.004 (.008)	-.005 (.008)
Rural		-.002 (.009)	-.006 (.009)
Prop. same ethnicity		.009 (.010)	-.016 (.013)
Prop. foreign-born		-.046 (.028)	-.033 (.032)
Prop. poor		-.081 (.030)**	-.035 (.027)
Ethnicity[h]			
Mexican			-.033 (.017)†
Cuban			-.022 (.022)
Puerto Rican			.003 (.018)
Other Hispanic			-.042 (.020)*
Chinese			.017 (.018)
Filipino			.008 (.021)
Other Asian			-.001 (.015)
African/Black			-.051 (.010)***
Constant	.796	.748	.761
R^2	.007	.034	.039

*** $p<.001$, ** $p<.01$, * $p<.05$, † $p<.10$ (two-tailed test)
[a]The square root of this variable is used to adjust for skewness. [b]Reference category is third and later generations. [c]Measured as mean deviation. [d]Conditionally relevant variable. For first generation immigrant youth, these variables test whether the effect of being foreign-born depends on the age at arrival. [e]Reference category is two-parent households. [f]Reference category is west. [g]Reference category is urban. [h]Reference category is European/White.

older age engage in less deviant behavior than their counterparts who immigrate at a younger age.

Overall, results for deviant behavior support the hypothesis that foreign-born youth are advantaged relative to native-born youth even after controlling for sociodemographic and community characteristics. As with depression and positive affect, however, much of the support for the hypothesis that second-generation youth are disadvantaged relative to third- and higher-generation youth are accounted for by sociodemographic factors, particularly parental education.

Physiological Response to Stress
Stress associated with the assimilation process may manifest not only as psychological problems, but also as physical health problems. The physiological response to stress index was constructed to address physical ailments that may be due to stress. Results indicate that, as with deviant behavior, first-generation youth have less physiological stress response than second-generation [$F(1,128)=7.89$, $p<.01$] and third- and higher-generation youth (Table 4.4). Confidence intervals indicate that the pattern of differences in means between the three immigrant generations is similar to that for depression and positive affect. The pattern is smaller differences in means between first- and second-generations, whereas third- and higher-generation youth have a mean level of physiological stress response that is largely different from the other two generations of youth. Unlike deviant behavior, however, controlling for sociodemographic and community factors reduce, rather than strengthen, the differences in physiological stress response between first-generation youth and youth of other generations. Although reduced, these differences remain statistically significant.

In contrast to results for depression, positive affect, and deviant behavior, the results for physiological stress response indicate that second-generation youth are advantaged, rather than disadvantaged, relative to third- and higher-generation youth. This lower physiological response to stress among second-generation youth, however, reduces to nonsignificance after controlling for sociodemographic and community factors. The ability of sociodemographic and community factors to explain differences between second-generation and third- and higher-generation youth, therefore, is similar for depression, positive affect, deviant behavior, and physiological stress response. In contrast to the other outcomes, however, level of neighborhood poverty seems to be the most influential in reducing differences between

Table 4.5. Ordered Logit of School Absence Due to Illness on Immigrant Generation

	Equation 1	Equation 2	Equation 3
1st generation[a]	-.227 (.115)†	-.500 (.140)***	-.453 (.131)**
2nd generation[a]	-.040 (.070)	-.157 (.087)†	-.153 (.097)
Generation pred	-.031 (.216)	-.600 (.258)*	-.612 (.256)*
Age[b]		.010 (.015)	.012 (.015)
Age at arrival[c]		-.004 (.021)	-.005 (.021)
Female		.428 (.041)***	.429 (.041)***
Family structure[d]			
Step-parent		.148 (.067)*	.145 (.067)*
One-parent		.205 (.064)**	.212 (.064)**
Other		.323 (.113)**	.330 (.113)**
English in home		.160 (.122)	.126 (.121)
Extended family		-.102 (.081)	-.098 (.081)
Household size		.029 (.015)†	.031 (.015)
Household income[b]		-.103 (.037)**	-.105 (.037)**
Parents' education[b]		-.036 (.009)***	-.034 (.010)**
Education predicted		.436 (.204)*	.434 (.204)*
Region[e]			
Midwest		-.213 (.073)**	-.202 (.072)**
South		-.339 (.080)***	-.324 (.079)***
Northeast		-.249 (.095)*	-.245 (.095)*
Residence[f]			
Suburb		-.150 (.062)*	-.145 (.062)*
Rural		-.288 (.073)***	-.290 (.072)***
Prop. same ethnicity		-.074 (.082)	-.151 (.102)
Prop. foreign-born		.239 (.247)	.268 (.241)
Prop. poor		.672 (.218)**	.751 (.224)**
Prop. predicted		-.592 (.235)*	-.599 (.237)*
Ethnicity[g]			
Mexican			-.059 (.101)
Cuban			-.023 (.398)
Puerto Rican			.160 (.166)
Other Hispanic			-.320 (.169)†
Chinese			-.394 (.210)†
Filipino			.157 (.215)
Other Asian			-.248 (.175)
African/Black			-.095 (.072)

continued on next page

Table 4.5 (cont'd)

	Equation 1	Equation 2	Equation 3
Cut points			
1	.639	.861	.780
2	2.984	3.247	3.167
3	4.393	4.663	4.583
4	5.382	5.654	5.574
F-statistic	1.33	10.41	8.82
Degrees of freedom	3, 126	25, 104	33, 96

*** $p<.001$, ** $p<.01$, * $p<.05$, † $p<.10$ (two-tailed test)
[a]Reference category is third and later generations. [b]Measured as mean deviation. [c]Conditionally relevant variable. For first generation immigrant youth, these variables test whether the effect of being foreign-born depends on the age at arrival. [d]Reference category is two-parent households. [e]Reference category is west. [f]Reference category is urban. [g]Reference category is European/White.

generations, rather than parental education and household income and size.

Table 4.4 also indicates that youth of African background and those who are of Other Hispanic background (i.e., neither Mexican, Cuban, nor Puerto Rican) have significantly less physiological response to stress than youth of European background. Males, youth residing in two-parent and larger size households, and youth who live in high poverty neighborhoods report lower physiological response.

These results support the hypothesis that foreign-born youth are in better health than native-born youth. Differences among native-born youth also provide support for the hypothesis that second-generation youth are in better health than third- and higher-generation youth, however, only at the bivariate level. This appears to support arguments that increased stressors that face the foreign-born as they assimilate into American society may manifest as physiological symptoms (Hernandez and Charney 1998).

Absence from School Due to Illness
Although there is a tendency for first-generation youth to have fewer absences due to illness than third- and higher-generation youth ($p=.05$) there is no difference in school absences between first- and second-generation or between second- and third- and higher-generation youth (Table 4.5). Confidence intervals further indicate that mean differences in absences across the three immigrant groups may be small. Statistically significant differences between first-generation youth and

Table 4.6. Overall Health[a] Regressed on Immigrant Generation

	Equation 1	Equation 2	Equation 3
1st generation[b]	.001 (.010)	.025 (.015)†	.042 (.015)**
2nd generation[b]	.001 (.009)	.003 (.009)	.013 (.009)
Generation pred	-.077 (.025)**	.001 (.040)	.007 (.041)
Age[c]		-.001 (.002)	-.002 (.001)
Age at arrival[d]		-.121E-4 (.002)	-.315E-3 (.002)
Female		-.038 (.005)***	-.039 (.005)***
Family structure[e]			
Step-parent		-.026 (.007)***	-.027 (.007)***
One-parent		-.021 (.008)*	-.025 (.008)**
Other		-.012 (.016)	-.018 (.016)
English in home		-.009 (.015)	-.016 (.015)
Extended family		-.011 (.010)	-.011 (.010)
Household size		-.001 (.002)	-.002 (.002)
Household income[c]		.011 (.006)†	.014 (.006)*
Parents' education[c]		.009 (.001)***	.008 (.001)***
Region[f]			
Midwest		.010 (.010)	.004 (.009)
South		.024 (.009)*	.014 (.009)
Northeast		.029 (.010)**	.023 (.011)*
Residence[g]			
Suburb		-.023 (.007)**	-.023 (.007)**
Rural		-.024 (.010)*	-.022 (.009)*
Prop. same ethnicity		.003 (.007)	.009 (.010)
Prop. foreign-born		-.017 (.026)	-.024 (.028)
Prop. poor		-.087 (.029)**	-.125 (.029)***
Ethnicity[h]			
Mexican			-.011 (.013)
Cuban			.031 (.020)
Puerto Rican			-.014 (.017)
Other Hispanic			.006 (.019)
Chinese			.005 (.023)
Filipino			-.048 (.022)*
Other Asian			-.037 (.021)†
African/Black			.038 (.008)***
Constant	1.954	2.009	2.021
R^2	.001	.036	.039

*** $p<.001$, ** $p<.01$, * $p<.05$, † $p<.10$ (two-tailed test)
[a]The square root of this variable is used to adjust for skewness. [b]Reference category is third and later generations. [c]Measured as mean deviation. [d]Conditionally relevant variable. For first generation immigrant youth, these variables test whether the effect of being foreign-born depends on the age at arrival. [e]Reference category is two-parent households. [f]Reference category is west. [g]Reference category is urban. [h]Reference category is European/White.

youth of other generations are only evident after controlling for sociodemographic and community factors.   Not only are first-generation youth significantly less likely to be absent than third- and higher-generation youth, results not shown here indicate they are also less likely to be absent than second-generation youth [$F(1,128)=6.38$, $p<.01$].   This seems to indicate that absences due to illness would be even lower among first-generation youth if not for their residency in high poverty neighborhoods and their low income and parental education.

These findings contrast sharply with those discussed previously in this chapter where the associations between immigrant generation and health and behavior outcomes are first established at the bivariate level. Further analyses not presented here indicate that first-generation youth have a 70.2 percent probability of no school absences.   Second-generation and third- and higher-generation youth have a 66.4 and 65.4 percent probability of no absences, respectively.   Table 4.5 also indicates that absences due to illness are less likely among males, youth in two-parent and high-income households, youth whose parents are more educated, and youth living in low poverty neighborhoods, non-urban neighborhoods, and non-Western regions of the country.

These results do not support the hypothesis of disadvantaged health.   Rather, the results provide some support for the opposite hypothesis with foreign-born youth reporting fewer absences from school due to illness after controlling for sociodemographic and community factors, particularly socioeconomic factors.   No significant difference is evident between second- and third- and higher-generation youth; thus, neither hypothesis comparing these groups is supported.

Overall Health
Overall health is a measure of adolescent self-rated health. Statistically significant differences in overall health between immigrant generations are only evident after controlling for sociodemographic factors, specifically ethnic background (Table 4.6).   Although first-generation youth report less physiological response to stress and tend to report fewer absences from school due to illness at the bivariate level, they do not consider themselves to be in better overall health than youth of other generations.   The similarity in mean levels of overall health across generations is further evident in the confidence intervals.

Adjustments for ethnic background result in a 68 percent increase in the first-generation coefficient such that first-generation youth are in significantly better overall health than third- and higher-generation youth. First-generation youth also report better overall health than second-generation youth [$F(1,128)=5.18$, $p<.05$]. This strengthened association, the greater overall health of youth of African background and poorer health of those of Filipino background relative to Whites, and the similarities between youth of other ethnic groups and Whites indicate that the overall health of first-generation youth would be even greater if the first-generation was made up of more Blacks and fewer Filipinos. There is no difference in overall health between second-generation and third- and higher-generation youth even after adjusting for ethnic background.

Similar to results for school absence due to illness, results for overall health support the hypothesis of a health advantage for foreign-born youth, but only after controlling for sociodemographic factors. Additionally, as with school absence, no significant difference is evident between second-generation and third- and higher-generation youth; thus, neither hypothesis with regard to these groups is supported.

OVERVIEW
Much of the research literature on adolescent immigrants finds that, contrary to intuitive expectations and those of classical assimilation theory, foreign-born youth are in better health and engage in less deviant behavior than youth born in the United States (e.g., Harker 2001; Harris 1999; Hernandez and Charney 1998). Researchers argue that findings of better health and behavior among the foreign-born that decline with time spent in the U.S. and across generations are not surprising given the high number of stressors they may encounter during the assimilation process (Hernandez and Charney 1998; Portes and Rumbaut 1996). Immigrant youth may be forced to deal with language problems, perceived discrimination, and intergenerational conflicts arising from variations in rates of assimilation by parents and their children. Additionally, living in poor inner-city neighborhoods often means that youth assimilate into that aspect of American society, thus, adopting the habits of people who are more likely to experience poor health and behavior.

Overall, these results indicate that foreign-born youth do tend to experience better health and behavior than native-born youth. This supports the findings of other researchers (e.g., Harker 2001; Harris 1999; Hernandez and Charney 1998); however, there appears to be distinct mental versus physical health differences. Foreign-born youth have less physiological response to stress, are less likely to be absent from school due to illness, and consider themselves to be in better overall health than native-born youth. These findings of better physical health for the foreign-born are evident after controlling for sociodemographic and community characteristics. In contrast to findings for physical health, results of analyses on depression and positive affect show worse health for foreign-born than for native-born youth. Much of these differences in mental health, however, disappear after controlling for factors related to socioeconomic status and household size. Findings for deviant behavior are similar to those for physical health in that foreign-born youth engage in less deviant behavior than native-born youth even after controlling for sociodemographic and community characteristics. The hypothesis of better health and behavior among the foreign-born than among the native-born, therefore, is supported for physical health and behavioral outcomes. Findings for depression and positive affect, however, do not support either hypothesis of better or worse health after controlling for sociodemographic and community factors, particularly household income, parental education, and household size.

Generally, these findings do not support either hypothesis of better or worse health and behavior among second-generation relative to third- and higher-generation youth. Rather, the two immigrant generations appear to be similar with much of the difference accounted for by factors related to socioeconomic status and household size. Among native-born youth, those with foreign-born parents are more depressed, and report less positive affect, more behavior problems, and less physiological stress response than youth with native-born parents. These relationships, however, are reduced to nonsignificance after controlling for sociodemographic and community factors.

Other Findings
Several other issues arise from these results. One issue is the findings for age at arrival in the U.S. Surprisingly, the results indicate that age at arrival is not associated with the health of foreign-born youth. There is an association with deviant behavior such that youth who arrived in the U.S. at a later age report less deviant behavior. The argument that age at arrival may impact adaptation is based on the idea that youth who arrived early in childhood are likely to be more similar to native-born youth than those who arrived later in childhood (Rumbaut 1994a). These findings provide little support for this argument.

Another issue is language. Language difficulties are considered a significant stressor for the foreign-born who are from non-English speaking countries. Whether or not English is the language usually spoken in the home has little effect on the association between immigrant generation and health and behavioral outcomes in this study.

Another issue is the disparity in the association between immigrant generation and depressive symptoms and that between immigrant generation and physiological stress response. Theoretically, depressive symptoms should be positively related to physiological stress response. The expression of physical symptoms is a sign of stress, as is psychological symptoms. Correlation analysis indicates that depression is positively associated with physiological stress response. In this study, analyses of the association between these outcomes and immigrant generation indicate that, although the foreign-born have higher levels of depressive symptoms, they also report less physiological stress response than native-born youth at the bivariate level. A possible explanation for this may be that the home environment protects them from the physical symptoms of stress by reducing the fear that tends to precede such symptoms. The factors that protect them from experiencing the physical symptoms, however, may also increase their depression. An example of this may be high parental control or restrictive parenting. Although such parenting may reduce the anxiety that youth may feel from having the responsibility of making their own choices, such control may also increase depression. A similar explanation may account for low positive affect among the foreign-born.

These results seem to support both arguments of decreased and increased well-being with time spent in the U.S. and across immigrant generations. Although many adults migrate to provide a better life for their children, in some respects the lives of their children may worsen due to the lifestyles to which they become assimilated and the stresses and unfulfilled expectations that may accompany the assimilation process.

CHAPTER 5

Family Process

Determining the relationship between immigrant generation and family process is the second step in ascertaining whether family process can help to explain the association between immigrant generation and health and behavior. Parent-child conflict, for example, will not help to explain findings of fewer physiological responses to stress among the foreign-born if foreign-born youth engage in greater conflict with parents. Five measures of family process are examined: independence in decision-making, parents' educational expectations for their children, parent-child closeness, parent-child conflict, and parental involvement in activities with their children. A measure of social support by parents, other adults, and peers is also examined. The broader term of family process is used because it reflects more than simply parent-child relationship.

Although there are reasons to expect that foreign-born and native-born youth differ with regard to family process, little research has addressed this question. The experiences of foreign-born youth may reflect what is often considered better or more adaptive family process within a Western cultural framework. Foreign-born youth may be in better health and report less deviant behavior because they are more closely supervised than native-born children. Youth who are recent immigrants may be closely supervised because they are new to the country and parents take extra care to ensure that their children are doing well. On the other hand, immigrant youth may be afforded little independence with regard to decision-making, which may both positively and negatively affect well-being. In addition, parent-child closeness and involvement may be higher among recent immigrants because they have few or no friends when they first arrive and so are almost forced to spend time, and engage in activities, together. Aspects of immigrant families may be considered maladaptive within a Western or mainstream cultural framework (Santisteban & Mitrani 2003). An example is a tendency towards larger immigrant households where parents' attention may be diluted because it has to be spread widely. Additionally, large immigrant households may include adults, other than parents, with whom youth may develop relationships that are similar to that of parent and child. Such relationships may reduce efforts to develop and sustain strong parent-child relations.

Family process may also explain why health and behavior changes across immigrant generations. Why might family process change? The migration process disrupts normal family life (Zhou 1997). In addition, during the assimilation process, immigrants are confronted with factors that contribute to acculturative stress and intergenerational conflict such as role reversals between parents and children due to parents' difficulties with a new language and culture. Another factor may be differences between parents' and children's perceptions of discrimination. These factors may result in a reduction in parental authority and increased parent-child conflict (Zhou 1997; Coll and Magnuson 1997). Changes in family process could also be due to differences between parents' and children's perceptions of American society. Immigrant children are often focused on fitting in with their peers while their parents are focused on maintaining traditional family life (Zhou 1997; Dublin 1996).

The few studies that have addressed the association between immigrant generation and family process have found some evidence of greater parental supervision of the foreign-born (Harker 2001; Chiu 1987) as well as weak evidence of increased parent-child closeness and social support (Harker 2001). Findings with regard to parent-child conflict are inconsistent. Rumbaut (1994a) found greater conflict among foreign-born and Harker (2001) found less conflict.

Given the combination of arguments outlined above and general research findings, results from this study may indicate that foreign-born youth have more adaptive family process and social support than native-born youth. There are counter arguments, however, that suggest that foreign-born youth may have less adaptive family process and social support than native-born youth. Both hypotheses are tested.

Differences in family process and social support among native-born youth are also examined.

ANALYTIC STRATEGY

Regression analyses are used to examine the association between immigrant generation and family process and social support. Cases whose generation status could not be determined are excluded from all analyses because the number is very small when family process measures are used as dependent variables.

The results of the regression analyses are outlined in Tables 5.1 to 5.6. The tables provide unstandardized coefficients with standard errors in brackets. Equation 1 of each table presents the bivariate association between immigrant generation and family process outcomes. Equation 2 adds controls for sociodemographic and community factors. Equation 3 includes controls for ethnic background.

RESULTS

Do foreign-born and native-born youth differ in family process and social support? The results are inconsistent and complex. Differences in family process and social support between foreign-born and native-born youth are not as distinct as differences in their health and behavior. Comparisons of first-generation and third- and higher-generation youth indicate that first-generation youth have lower independence in decision-making, lower parent-child closeness, lower parental involvement, and are less likely to experience parent-child conflict than third- and higher-generation youth. Differences in parent-child closeness, parental involvement, and parent-child conflict are reduced to nonsignificance after adjusting for various sociodemographic and community factors, particularly income, parental education, neighborhood poverty, and household size. In contrast, first-generation youth have higher parental expectations for education than third- and higher-generation youth net of sociodemographic and community factors.

Differences between first- and second-generation youth are also evident, but the differences are far fewer and do not always parallel those for first-generation and third- and higher-generation youth. Generally, there are more findings that indicate less, rather than more, adaptive family process among first-generation relative to third- and higher-generation youth; however, there are more findings of similar,

Table 5.1.   Independence in Decision-Making Regressed on Immigrant Generation

	Equation 1	Equation 2	Equation 3
1st generation[a]	-.056 (.017)**	-.041 (.012)**	-.041 (.014)**
2nd generation[a]	-.035 (.012)**	-.017 (.009)†	-.018 (.010)†
Age[b]		.045 (.002)***	.045 (.002)***
Age at arrival[c]		-.007 (.003)*	-.006 (.003)*
Female		.006 (.004)	.006 (.004)
Family structure[d]			
Step-parent		.005 (.007)	.005 (.006)
One-parent		.027 (.007)***	.029 (.006)***
Other		.015 (.015)	.018 (.015)
English in home		.015 (.014)	.017 (.012)
Extended family		.013 (.009)	.012 (.009)
Household size		-.009 (.002)***	-.009 (.001)***
Household income[b]		.014 (.005)**	.014 (.005)**
Parents' education[b]		.002 (.001)*	.002 (.001)*
Education predicted		.019 (.028)	.020 (.028)
Region[e]			
Midwest		-.001 (.013)	-.002 (.013)
South		-.013 (.012)	-.013 (.012)
Northeast		.005 (.015)	.005 (.015)
Residence[f]			
Suburb		.005 (.007)	.005 (.008)
Rural		.003 (.010)	.001 (.010)
Prop. same ethnicity		.005 (.009)	-.007 (.011)
Prop. foreign-born		-.016 (.042)	-.029 (.049)
Prop. poor		-.095 (.027)**	-.073 (.028)**
Ethnicity[g]			
Mexican			-.013 (.014)
Cuban			.047 (.035)
Puerto Rican			-.003 (.018)
Other Hispanic			-.014 (.022)
Chinese			.013 (.027)
Filipino			-.013 (.019)
Other Asian			.002 (.021)
African/Black			-.021 (.010)*
Constant	.738	-.017	-.013
R^2	.005	.153	.154

*** p<.001, ** p<.01, * p<.05, † p<.10 (two-tailed test)
[a]Reference category is third and later generations. [b]Measured as mean deviation. [c]Conditionally relevant variable. [d]Reference category is two-parent households. [e]Reference category is west. [f]Reference category is urban. [g]Reference category is European/White.

rather than different, family process between first- and second-generation youth. Generally, with the exception of parental expectations for education and parent-child conflict, the family process of foreign-born youth appear to be less adaptive than, or similar to, that of native-born youth.

Differences in family process between second-generation and third- and higher generation youth are somewhat inconsistent. Many of the findings, however, indicate that second-generation and third- and higher-generation youth tend to have similar levels of parent-child closeness, parent-child conflict, parental expectations for education, and parental involvement at bivariate and multivariate levels. Generally, there is more research support for similar levels of family process, than for significant differences, contrary to what was hypothesized. Surprisingly, findings indicate no significant association between immigrant generation and social support.

Independence in Decision-Making
Independence in decision-making serves to monitor and control children's behavior. The bivariate results in Table 5.1 indicate that first- and second-generation youth report less independence in decision-making than third- and higher-generation youth. There is no difference in independence between first- and second-generation youth.

Sociodemographic and community factors account for some of the difference in independence in decision-making between first-generation and third- and higher-generation immigrant youth while eliminating the significant difference between second-generation and third- and higher-generation youth. The coefficient representing the first-generation shows a 27 percent decline from equation 1. Table 5.1 also indicates that, among first-generation youth, an older age at arrival is associated with less independence in decision-making. Less independence in decision-making is also indicated for youth residing in large households, those living in poor neighborhoods, and those who are black or of African background.

These findings support the hypothesis that foreign-born youth are afforded less independence in their decision-making than native-born youth, particularly native-born youth with native-born parents. The results also support the hypothesis that among native-born youth, those with foreign-born parents tend to have less independence than those with native-born parents. Surprisingly, ethnic background does not

Table 5.2. Parental Expectations for Education Regressed on Immigrant Generation

	Equation 1	Equation 2	Equation 3
1st generation[a]	.127 (.053)*	.216 (.060)***	.190 (.064)**
2nd generation[a]	.004 (.038)	.010 (.040)	.011 (.041)
Age[b]		-.031 (.006)***	.033 (.006)***
Age at arrival[c]		.006 (.008)	.005 (.008)
Female		.034 (.019)†	.033 (.019)†
Family structure[d]			
Step-parent		-.072 (.028)*	-.071 (.028)*
One-parent		.020 (.034)	.009 (.035)
Other		-.189 (.069)**	-.201 (.070)**
English in home		-.096 (.059)	-.123 (.058)*
Extended family		.039 (.038)	.037 (.038)
Household size		-.017 (.008)*	-.019 (.008)*
Household income[b]		.113 (.015)***	.116 (.015)***
Parents' education[b]		.047 (.005)***	.045 (.005)***
Region[e]			
Midwest		.143 (.053)**	.144 (.055)*
South		.143 (.052)**	.141 (.055)*
Northeast		.135 (.056)*	.130 (.060)*
Residence[f]			
Suburb		-.035 (.031)	-.044 (.031)
Rural		-.057 (.039)	-.059 (.040)
Prop. same ethnicity		-.079 (.035)*	-.035 (.050)
Prop. foreign-born		.082 (.106)	.142 (.117)
Prop. poor		-.221 (.101)*	-.311 (.108)**
Ethnicity[g]			
Mexican			-.027 (.065)
Cuban			-.147 (.080)†
Puerto Rican			.001 (.111)
Other Hispanic			.023 (.065)
Chinese			.063 (.078)
Filipino			.107 (.095)
Other Asian			.086 (.087)
African/Black			.092 (.037)*
Constant	4.307	3.900	3.942
R^2	.001	.057	.058

*** p<.001, ** p<.01, * p<.05, † p<.10 (two-tailed test)
[a]Reference category is third and later generations. [b]Measured as mean deviation.
[c]Conditionally relevant variable. [d]Reference category is two-parent households.
[e]Reference category is west. [f]Reference category is urban. [g]Reference category is European/White.

have much effect. Research has found that, for example, Chinese parents tend to impose stricter rules on their children than Chinese American or European American parents (Chiu 1987). These results do not show evidence of differences in independence between European and Asian or Hispanic youth. Only youth of African background show evidence of less independence in decision-making than youth of European background.

Parental Expectations for Education
Although foreign-born youth have less independence in decision-making, they have greater parental expectations for education. Table 5.2 indicates that first-generation youth have greater educational expectations placed upon them by their parents than do second-generation [$F(1,128)=5.58$, $p<.05$] and third- and higher-generation youth. The effect of adjusting for sociodemographic and community factors is the reverse of that for independence—differences in expectations between first-generation youth and youth of other generations are strengthened, rather than reduced, by sociodemographic and community controls. There is no significant difference in educational expectations between second-generation and third- and higher-generation youth even after controlling for sociodemographic and community characteristics.

Table 5.2 also indicates that parental expectations are lower for older youth, those in step-parent and other households, those who usually speak English in the home, those living in larger size households and those living in poorer neighborhoods. Youth of African background experience greater educational expectation than youth of European background.

These results support the hypothesis of greater parental expectations for foreign-born youth compared to native-born youth. This seems to indicate that a frequent reason for immigrating to the United States is at play—parents' desire for a better education and a better life for their children. The large difference in expectations between first- and second-generation and the lack of difference between second-generation and third- and higher-generation youth indicate that this desire is especially strong among first-generation or more recent immigrants. The lack of a significant difference between the second-generation and third- and higher-generation youth does not support the hypotheses. It does seem to support arguments that factors related to acculturative stress and intergenerational conflict during the

Table 5.3. Parent-Child Closeness Regressed on Immigrant Generation

	Equation 1	Equation 2	Equation 3
1st generation[a]	-.082 (.031)**	-.028 (.038)	-.022 (.041)
2nd generation[a]	-.025 (.022)	-.019 (.023)	-.012 (.024)
Age[b]		-.053 (.004)***	-.054 (.004)***
Age at arrival[c]		-.004 (.005)	-.004 (.005)
Female		-.104 (.013)***	-.105 (.013)***
Family structure[d]			
Step-parent		-.175 (.017)***	-.176 (.017)***
One-parent		-.035 (.020)†	-.039 (.020)†
Other		-.125 (.041)**	-.131 (.041)**
English in home		-.006 (.037)	-.016 (.037)
Extended family		.041 (.023)†	.042 (.023)†
Household size		-.018 (.004)***	-.019 (.004)***
Household income[b]		-.004 (.012)	-.003 (.012)
Parents' education[b]		.007 (.003)*	.007 (.003)*
Education predicted		-.211 (.082)*	-.210 (.081)*
Region[e]			
Midwest		.030 (.026)	.025 (.027)
South		.071 (.022)**	.064 (.023)**
Northeast		.091 (.025)**	.082 (.027)**
Residence[f]			
Suburb		-.016 (.016)	-.017 (.017)
Rural		-.006 (.019)	-.004 (.020)
Prop. same ethnicity		.010 (.023)	.015 (.028)
Prop. foreign-born		-.027 (.056)	-.019 (.065)
Prop. poor		.132 (.073)†	.101 (.074)
Ethnicity[g]			
Mexican			-.020 (.030)
Cuban			-.028 (.044)
Puerto Rican			.013 (.053)
Other Hispanic			.017 (.047)
Chinese			-.133 (.077)†
Filipino			-.011 (.046)
Other Asian			.003 (.057)
African/Black			.027 (.020)
Constant	4.443	5.29	5.31
R^2	.001	.055	.055

*** p<.001, ** p<.01, * p<.05, † p<.10 (two-tailed test)
[a]Reference category is third and later generations. [b]Measured as mean deviation.
[c]Conditionally relevant variable. [d]Reference category is two-parent households.
[e]Reference category is west. [f]Reference category is urban. [g]Reference category is European/White.

assimilation process may serve to diminish parents' expectations for their children, especially the expectations of foreign-born parents with native-born children.

Parent-Child Closeness

Parent-child closeness is a measure of how close youth feel toward their parents and their level of satisfaction with their relationship with their parents. Table 5.3 indicates that, like independence in decision-making, foreign-born youth are less close to their parents than third- and higher-generation youth. First-generation youth also tend to have lower parent-child closeness than second-generation youth. Although differences in independence between immigrant generations are strengthened after controlling for sociodemographic and community factors, differences in parent-child closeness are reduced to nonsignificance. Further analyses not shown here indicate that the lower parent-child closeness of first-generation youth is mainly due to their larger household size, lower parental education, and older age relative to third- and higher-generation youth.

Whereas second-generation youth tend to have lower independence in decision-making than third- and higher-generation youth, no significant difference in parent-child closeness is evident between these two generations of immigrant youth. Table 5.3 indicates that youth in step-parent and other households report being less close to their parents, as do those who are older, female, and reside in larger households.

In contrast to findings for independence and educational expectations, these findings fail to strongly support the hypotheses. Although first-generation youth tend to be less close to their parents than youth of other immigrant generations, this difference is largely due to first-generation youth's lower parental education and higher household size and age. The bivariate result indicating less closeness among foreign-born youth than youth of other immigrant generations is not particularly surprising and is similar to that reported by Harker (2001). Additionally, findings of lower closeness among the foreign-born are not surprising given: (1) their larger household size where the likelihood of low parental attention is increased; and (2) their lower level of independence in decision-making, which may signify a lack of trust and thus hamper the development or sustainment of high parent-child closeness, especially among adolescents. Foreign-born youth may also experience lower closeness because they are more

Table 5.4. Logistic Regression of Parent-Child Conflict on Immigrant Generation

	Equation 1	Equation 2	Equation 3
1st generation[a]	-.290 (.096)**	-.246 (.129)†	-.217 (.132)
2nd generation[a]	.024 (.068)	.014 (.082)	.008 (.083)
Age		-.001 (.015)	-.003(.015)
Age at arrival[c]		-.013 (.020)	-.012 (.012)
Female		.289 (.043)***	.295(.043)***
Family structure[d]			
Step-parent		.115 (.060)†	.113 (.061)†
One-parent		-.128 (.069)†	-.87 (.069)
Other		-.494 (.122)***	-.446 (.123)***
English in home		.154 (.096)	.203 (.097)*
Extended family		-.027 (.080)	-.023(.079)
Household size		-.011 (.014)	-.004 (.014)
Household income[b]		-.045 (.045)	-.059 (.045)
Parents' education[b]		-.005 (.010)	.482E-3 (.011)
Region[e]			
Midwest		-.043 (.079)	-.025 (.079)
South		-.155 (.067)*	-.123 (.068)†
Northeast		-.048 (.088)	-.026 (.088)
Residence[f]			
Suburb		.011 (.048)	.028 (.048)
Rural		.083 (.093)	.075 (.095)
Prop. same ethnicity		-.212 (.071)**	-.412 (.108)***
Prop. foreign-born		.016 (.286)	.023 (.289)
Prop. poor		-.651 (.223)**	-.307 (.244)
Ethnicity[g]			
Mexican			-.064 (.139)
Cuban			-.071 (.231)
Puerto Rican			-.041 (.153)
Other Hispanic			-.252 (.156)
Chinese			-.287 (.222)
Filipino			-.206 (.145)
Other Asian			-.218 (.181)
African/Black			-.389 (.094)***
Constant	-.479	-.108	-.146
F-statistic	5.24	4.47	5.17
Degrees of Freedom	2, 127	24, 105	32, 97

*** $p < .001$, ** $p < .01$, * $p < .05$, † $p < .10$ (two-tailed test)
[a]Reference category is third and later generations. [b]Measured as mean deviation. [c]Conditionally relevant variable. [d]Reference category is two-parent households. [e]Reference category is west. [f]Reference category is urban. [g]Reference category is European/White.

focused on fitting in with peers while parents are more focused on maintaining, for example, the cultural norms of their home country.

Parent-Child Conflict

Logistic regression is used to examine the association between adolescent immigrant generation and parent-child conflict. Table 5.4 indicates that, despite low levels of closeness and low independence in decision-making, first-generation youth are less likely to experience parent-child conflict than third- and higher-generation youth. Controlling for sociodemographic and community factors reduce the difference in parent-child conflict to nonsignificance. The lower probability of conflict among first-generation than third- and higher-generation youth appears to be largely due to ethnic background and residence in higher poverty neighborhoods.

Further analyses not presented here indicate that first-generation youth are also less likely to experience parent-child conflict than second-generation youth [F(1,128)=5.05, p<.01]. This tendency remains even after controlling for sociodemographic and community factors. The strength of the difference in the probability of conflict between first- and second-generation youth is similar to that for parents' educational expectations. Any significant differences between these two generations of immigrant youth with regard to other measures of family process tend to disappear after controlling for sociodemographic and community factors. Results indicate no difference in the probability of parent-child conflict between second-generation and third- and higher-generation youth. Table 5.4 also indicates that males, youth who reside in neighborhoods with a large proportion of persons who are the same ethnicity as them, youth who reside in households where English is usually spoken, and youth of African background are less likely to experience parent-child conflict.

These results partially support the hypothesis that foreign-born youth are less likely to experience parent-child conflict than other youth. Although sociodemographic factors explain the foreign-born's lower probability of conflict relative to second-generation youth, such factors do not entirely explain foreign-born youth's lower likelihood of conflict relative to third- and higher-generation youth. The results of the few studies that have examined parent-child conflict among immigrants have been mixed. These results support those of Harker (2001) and are contrary to Rumbaut (1994a). The finding of less conflict among the foreign-born could be considered surprising

Table 5.5. Parental Involvement Regressed on Immigrant Generation

	Equation 1	Equation 2	Equation 3
1st generation[a]	-.335 (.100)**	-.155 (.128)	-.059 (.132)
2nd generation[a]	-.144 (.090)	-.153 (.086)†	-.112 (.086)
Age1[b]		-.090 (.014)***	-.090 (.014)***
Age at arrival[c]		-.024 (.017)	-.023 (.017)
Female		.423 (.045)***	.423 (.045)***
Family structure[d]			
Step-parent		-.309 (.057)***	-.313 (.057)***
One-parent		-.381 (.068)***	-.389 (.067)***
Other		-.243 (.116)*	-.254 (.116)*
English in home		-.399 (.103)***	-.370 (.109)**
Extended family		.011 (.071)	.027 (.072)
Household size		-.018 (.015)	-.021 (.015)
Household income[b]		.200 (.046)***	.201 (.047)***
Income predicted		-.107 (.047)*	-.104 (.048)*
Parents' education[b]		.101 (.008)***	.104 (.008)***
Education predicted		-.789 (.185)***	-.800 (.183)***
Region[e]			
Midwest		.014 (.098)	.007 (.099)
South		.123 (.091)	.113 (.093)
Northeast		-.076 (.107)	-.099 (.113)
Residence[f]			
Suburb		-.089 (.064)	-.071 (.066)
Rural		.193 (.095)*	.214 (.096)*
Prop. same ethnicity		-.101 (.078)	-.097 (.114)
Prop. foreign-born		-.310 (.213)	-.153 (.247)
Prop. poor		-.632 (.231)**	-.672 (.266)*
Ethnicity[g]			
Mexican			.075 (.128)
Cuban			-.430 (.333)
Puerto Rican			.124 (.168)
Other Hispanic			-.010 (.158)
Chinese			-.367 (.223)
Filipino			-.433 (.138)**
Other Asian			-.144 (.201)
African/Black			.026 (.080)
Constant	4.037	3.941	3.86
R^2	.002	.083	.084

*** p<.001, ** p<.01, * p<.05, † p<.10 (two-tailed test)
[a]Reference category is third and later generations. [b]Measured as mean deviation. [c]Conditionally relevant variable. [d]Reference category is two-parent households. [e]Reference category is west. [f]Reference category is urban. [g]Reference category is European/White.

given the likelihood of acculturative stress among immigrant youth and earlier reported findings of less independence in decision-making and lower parent-child closeness among foreign-born youth. Restrictive childrearing practices and lack of autonomy are frequently associated with parent-child conflict (Collins and Luebker 1994). A lower probability of conflict, however, appears to be largely due to the poorer neighborhoods in which foreign-born youth reside. One possible explanation for the lower likelihood of conflict among those in poorer neighborhoods may be that the level of contact between parents and their children is reduced in high poverty neighborhoods, therefore, the opportunities for conflict are reduced. There may also be less conflict among the foreign-born if their culture emphasizes and promotes respect for elders.

Parental Involvement
Parent involvement assesses the extent to which youth and their parents engage in activities together. Table 5.4 indicates that the association between immigrant generation and involvement is very similar to the association with parent-child closeness. Parents of first-generation youth are significantly less involved with their children than parents of third- and higher-generation youth. Controlling for sociodemographic and community characteristics reduces this association to nonsignificance. Further analyses reveal that the lower parental involvement among first-generation youth is largely due to their lower household income and parental education. Differences between other immigrant generations are nonsignificant.

Table 5.5 also indicates that females, younger adolescents, those in two-parent households, those who reside in households where English is not usually spoken, those with higher household income, those whose parents are more educated, those living in rural areas, and those living in higher income neighborhoods report more parental involvement.

These results find only weak support for the hypothesis of lower parental involvement among foreign-born youth. This lower involvement, however, is largely due to the lower socioeconomic status of the foreign-born. Hypothesized differences in parental involvement between second-generation and third- and higher-generation youth are not supported. Results reveal that second-generation and third- and higher-generation youth share similar levels of parental involvement. These findings are very similar to those for parent-child closeness.

78 *Health and Behavior Among Immigrant Youth*

Table 5.6. Social Support Regressed on Immigrant Generation

	Equation 1	Equation 2	Equation 3
1st generation[a]	.034 (.033)	.029 (.046)	.046 (.047)
2nd generation[a]	.022 (.028)	-.012 (.025)	-.005 (.028)
Age[b]		-.061 (.005)***	-.062 (.004)***
Age at arrival[c]		-.005 (.006)	-.006 (.006)
Female		.018 (.014)	.017 (.014)
Family structure[d]			
Step-parent		-.141 (.016)***	-.142 (.016)***
One-parent		-.120 (.018)***	-.128 (.018)***
Other		-.066 (.032)*	-.075 (.031)*
English in home		-.061 (.039)	-.067 (.037)†
Extended family		-.018 (.022)	-.016 (.021)
Household size		-.012 (.004)**	-.014 (.004)**
Household income[b]		.013 (.012)	.015 (.012)
Parents' education[b]		.007 (.003)*	.007 (.003)*
Education predicted		-.256 (.078)**	-.258 (.078)**
Region[e]			
Midwest		.023 (.037)	.025 (.038)
South		.074 (.036)*	.072 (.038)†
Northeast		.087 (.041)*	.089 (.043)*
Residence[f]			
Suburb		-.016 (.021)	-.014 (.022)
Rural		.013 (.031)	.019 (.031)
Prop. same ethnicity		.020 (.024)	.044 (.031)
Prop. foreign-born		.130 (.103)	.142 (.108)
Prop. poor		.111 (.082)	.056 (.086)
Ethnicity[g]			
Mexican			.044 (.037)
Cuban			-.062 (.075)
Puerto Rican			.016 (.054)
Other Hispanic			.020 (.048)
Chinese			-.072 (.099)
Filipino			.027 (.059)
Other Asian			-.064 (.060)
African/Black			.056 (.022)*
Constant	4.007	4.907	4.90
R^2	.3E-3	.057	.059

*** p<.001, ** p<.01, * p<.05, † p<.10 (two-tailed test)
[a]Reference category is third and later generations. [b]Measured as mean deviation. [c]Conditionally relevant variable. [d]Reference category is two-parent households. [e]Reference category is west. [f]Reference category is urban. [g]Reference category is European/White.

Social Support
The measure of social support used in these analyses includes support from parents, other adults, and peers. In contrast to the other variables examined in this chapter, the results for social support indicate no significant differences among immigrant generations (Table 5.6). The addition of controls for sociodemographic and community factors has no impact on the association between immigrant generation and social support.

Social support is considered a particularly important resource for immigrant children because their experience is often a stressful one. These results, however, indicate no statistically significant difference between first-, second-, and third- and higher-generations in their level of perceived social support. These findings do not support the hypotheses. As with Harker's (2001) findings, there is only a tendency for first-generation youth to report higher social support, but the difference is not significant. These findings may indicate that networks of support for immigrant youth are not as strong as those for adult immigrants, the focus of much of the research on immigrant social support.

OVERVIEW
Foreign-born youth may have more adaptive family process than native-born youth because they are fairly new to the country and so their parents provide more attention and support. On the other hand, foreign-born youth may have less adaptive family process because they may not have wanted to immigrate and because they may reside in large households where parents have difficulty providing their children with equal amounts of attention.

Results indicate that the association between immigrant generation and family process and social support is complex. On the one hand, parents of foreign-born youth allow their children less independence to make their own decisions and hold higher educational expectations for their adolescent children than native-born parents. These associations appear to be the strongest given that they remain even after adjusting for sociodemographic and community characteristics. Additionally, foreign-born youth are less involved with their parents and experience less parent-child closeness. Despite these findings, foreign-born youth are less likely to engage in conflicts with their parents than are native-born youth with native-born parents. The lower socioeconomic status and larger household size of foreign-born youth are mostly responsible for their lower levels of parental involvement and parent-child closeness. Social support, as measured here, does not significantly vary across the three immigrant generations of youth.

These results only partially support the hypotheses. There is some support for the hypothesis that foreign-born youth enjoy more adaptive family process than native-born youth, but only with respect to greater parental expectations for education and less parent-child conflict. Findings for independence in decision-making, parental involvement, and parent-child closeness provide some support for the hypothesis that foreign-born youth have less adaptive family process than native-born youth. The issue of parenting styles among immigrants and non-immigrants is examined within the context of a Western cultural framework. Family process that may be considered less adaptive within a mainstream or majority culture may be adaptive within other cultures. As such, differences in parenting and family process between immigrants and non-immigrants often do not reflect deficits or ineffective parenting. Rather, differences may simply reflect the diversity in effective parenting styles across cultures.

There is little support for the hypotheses of significant differences between second-generation and third- and higher-generation youth. The only significant finding is that second- generation youth tend to have less independence in their decision-making than third- and higher-generation youth. The home lives of second-generation and third- and higher-generation youth, thus, appear to be similar. More frequent struggles for control and conflict seem to occur between native-born youth and their foreign-born parents than between foreign-born youth and foreign-born parents. This seems to support the acculturative stress argument that perceived incompatibilities between new and old cultures may negatively influence family process.

Several other findings from these analyses are noteworthy. One such finding is the relatively small association between extended family households and family process. Extended family household is associated with higher parent-child closeness, but is not related to any other measure of family process. Another is the relatively small difference in family process between youth of European background and those of other ethnic backgrounds. Much of the significant differences occur between youth of African and European backgrounds. Youth of Filipino background are the only other group that is significantly different from youth of European background—youth of

Filipino background experience less parental involvement than their European counterparts.

Establishing the relationships between immigrant generation and family process and social support is an important step prior to addressing the research question: Does family process and social support help to explain the association between immigrant generation and health and behavioral outcomes? The results outlined in this chapter will be used to examine this question.

CHAPTER 6

Mental Health and Behavior

This chapter focuses on the question of whether measures of family process help to explain the association between adolescent immigrant generation status and depression, positive affect, and deviant behavior. The results of analyses outlined in the previous two chapters will be used to frame the analyses to address this larger question.

The literature on adolescent psychological well-being identifies two categories of psychological disorders: internalizing and externalizing disorders. Internalizing disorders are those such as depression and anxiety that are more disturbing to the children who have such disorders than to other individuals. Externalizing disorders, such as conduct disorder and attention deficit hyperactivity disorder, are more disturbing to others than to the children who suffer from such disorders (American Psychiatric Association 1987). Children who exhibit internalizing and externalizing problems have been referred to as troubled and troublesome children, respectively (Shamsie 1995). Deviant behavior as defined here shares some of the symptoms of conduct disorder, a condition defined by the American Psychiatric Association as a "persistent pattern of conduct in which the basic rights of others and major age-appropriate societal norms or rules are violated" (American Psychiatric Association 1987:53). Conduct disorder often manifests as, for example, lying, stealing, physical aggression, cheating, and truancy (American Psychiatric Association 1987). Although the measure of deviant behavior used in this study does not meet the diagnostic standards required for conduct disorder, it includes some of the same behaviors. In this chapter, depression and positive affect (negative affect is really the disturbance aspect of this measure) are internalizing behaviors and the deviant behavior measure is the externalizing behavior. This allows for a more clear contrast between the two types of behavior, particularly as the next chapter, Chapter 7, will address physical health outcomes.

BACKGROUND

It is well known that family factors are associated with the well-being of children and adolescents. The family is one of the most important agents of socialization in children's lives. Researchers have found that factors related to family process such as high parental supervision, low parent-child conflict, and high levels of closeness between parents and children might have protective influences on well-being (Patten et al. 1997; Rumbaut 1994a; Dornbusch 1989; Marjoribanks 1987; Steinberg 1986). If adolescent immigrant generations also differ in family process, as indicated in Chapter 5, it is not difficult to postulate that family process may help to explain differences in well-being among foreign-born youth with foreign-born parents, native-born youth with foreign-born parents, and native-born youth with native-born parents. The assimilation process may exaggerate differences between parents and children that may affect parent-child relationship, and family process overall. One of the differences that may be exaggerated is a gap in cultural norms, with parents wanting to adhere to tradition and youth wanting to conform to American norms. An example of a gap between parents and children is the value of engaging in parent-child activities. Foreign-born parents may consider it important that the entire family have dinner together or go to the movies together; however, foreign-born youth who have lived in the U.S. for a significant period of time or native-born youth with foreign-born parents may consider doing such things, especially going to the movies, as a source of embarrassment, particularly if the parent does not speak English properly or act un-American in the eyes of their children. This, coupled with other reasons why average adolescents are embarrassed by their parents, places increased stress on the parent-child relationship. It is conceivable that differences in levels of parent-child activities among youth of different generations due to scenarios such as the one just outlined could influence adolescent health risk behavior (spending time with delinquent friends or staying home all the time and developing feelings of depression) and ultimately health. Youth could choose to socialize with delinquent friends and imitate their behavior.

Parent-child differences exaggerated by the assimilation process may also lead to intergenerational conflict and the eroding of parental authority. Circumstances in which children act as interpreters for parents who have difficulty with the English language have been identified as a key factor in the eroding of parental authority (Zhou 1997; Coll and Magnuson 1997). Differences in cultural norms related to child discipline may also strain the parent-child relationship (Waters 1997). Youth who experience poor family process due to these factors may be lacking in what has been identified as protective factors and so may be more susceptible to poor health and behavior.

As the associations between immigrant generation and depressive symptoms as well as positive affect are already explained by sociodemographic factors, family process is not expected to have any explanatory influence on these associations. Family process, however, is expected to significantly moderate the association between immigrant generation and depression and between generation and positive affect with first-generation youth being less negatively affected by poorer family process. With regard to deviant behavior, family process is expected to reduce differences in deviant behavior between first-generation youth and youth of other immigrant generations.

ANALYTIC STRATEGY
The analytic approach is based on the results presented in the previous two chapters. The results presented in Chapter 4 outline the association between immigrant generation and health and behavioral outcomes. Foreign-born youth report more depression, less positive affect, and less deviant behavior than native-born youth. Chapter 5 outlined the association between immigrant generation and family process. Foreign-born youth are found to report greater parental expectations for education, and less parent-child conflict, parent-child closeness, independence in decision-making, and parental involvement. In summarizing these relationships in this chapter, significant associations from bivariate and multivariate analyses are used. For example, greater depression among the foreign-born, compared to the native-born, is a bivariate relationship. This relationship becomes nonsignificant after controlling for sociodemographic and community characteristics. Foreign-born youth are referred to as more depressed because that is the basic relationship as well as the significant relationship in the analyses that have so far been reported on the association between immigrant generation and depression. The family process measures are

based on this significant relationship. The same applies to measures of family process, in that, for example, foreign-born youth are referred to here as being less close to their parents although this is a bivariate relationship that is reduced to nonsignificance after controlling for sociodemographic and community factors. This strategy reflects the basic relationship and is used to test the influence of parent-child closeness on the relationship between immigrant generation and health outcomes.

Although sociodemographic characteristics largely explain the higher depression and lower positive affect of foreign-born relative to native-born youth, these outcomes are included in this chapter to determine if family process alters the larger association between immigrant generation and health and behavior. The association between independence in decision-making and health, for example, may vary by immigrant generation. Although family process will not help to explain the association between immigrant generation and depression or immigrant generation and positive affect, it may offer important insights into how immigrant generations differ.

Results from the previous two chapters are used to determine which aspects of family process may affect the associations between immigrant generation and depression, positive affect, and deviant behavior. As stated above, foreign-born youth report greater depressive symptoms, less positive affect, and less deviant behavior than native-born youth. The foreign-born, therefore, seems to have more internalizing problems (depression and negative affect) and less externalizing problems (deviant behavior). Foreign-born youth also report greater parental expectations for education, and less parent-child conflict, parent-child closeness, independence in decision-making, and parental involvement than native-born youth. Given these findings, family process measures on which foreign-born youth may be considered more lacking (namely, independence in decision-making, parent-child closeness, and parental involvement) are likely to be more associated with the health outcomes on which they are disadvantaged (e.g., depressive symptoms and positive affect) than other measures of family process. Similarly, these other measures of family process on which foreign-born youth may be considered advantaged (high parental expectations for education and low parent-child conflict) are likely to be more associated with the health and behavioral outcomes on which they are advantaged (e.g., deviant behavior). This is the strategy that is used to analyze the role of family process in the associations between immigrant generation and depressive symptoms, positive affect, and deviant behavior. Social support is not included in this or remaining chapters because no significant differences are evident by immigrant generation (see Chapter 5).

In addition to choosing parent-child relation measures on which the foreign-born are advantaged to help explain health and behavioral outcomes on which the foreign-born are also advantaged, it is also important to use parent-child measures that are significantly and appropriately (i.e., in the right direction) associated with health and behavior outcomes. The equation used to examine the effect of family process on the association between immigrant generation and deviant behavior includes not only expectations for education and parent-child conflict on which the foreign-born are advantaged, but also independence in decision-making. Independence in decision-making is included because lower independence is associated with less deviant behavior. For the correlations between family process and health and behavior measures, please see Table A.2 in the Appendix.

Results are based on regression analyses and are outlined in Tables 6.1 to 6.3. The tables may be considered an extension of those presented in Chapter 4 (specifically, Tables 4.1 to 4.3) or they may be considered individually. To facilitate the latter purpose, the first equation in each of the tables is the same as the last equation in the equivalent table in Chapter 4 – i.e., the first equation in Table 6.1 is the same as the last equation in Table 4.1, the first equation in Table 6.2 is the same as the last equation in Table 4.2, and so on. The first equation represents the outcome variable regressed on immigrant generation, sociodemographic and community characteristics, and ethnic background. As they are not significantly associated with the outcomes presented in this chapter, variables related to region of the country, language spoken in the home, and the presence of extended family in the household are not presented in the tables. Relevant family process measures are included in equation 2. Although variables are included to adjust for whether or not the family process measures are imputed, the tables include only those variables that are significant. This strategy reduces clutter in the tables, as between five and six of these imputed/nonimputed dummy variables are used to control for cases missing specific family process values (see the analysis section of Chapter 3).

The final equation includes significant interaction terms. These interaction terms are the result of analyses to determine how the significance of age, sex, household income, parental education, ethnic background, and family process vary by immigrant generation. These interactions are examined because it is reasonable to expect that the effect of age, for example, may vary by immigrant generation given that younger and older adolescents often have different experiences that may affect their health and behavior. Diverse experiences are also at issue for males versus females, those of various income and educational levels, and those of various ethnic backgrounds. The interactions for each of these variables are examined in separate models. The significant interactions from these separate models are then combined into a unified model and presented in equation 3.

RESULTS

Although the higher level of depressive symptoms and lower positive affect of first- and second-generation relative to third- and higher-generation youth are explained by sociodemographic factors, particularly parental education and household income and size, family process has significant influences on the associations. First, results indicate that adjusting for family process changes the nature of the association between immigrant generation and depression such that first-generation youth are now less depressed than third- and higher-generation youth. First-generation youth, therefore, would have less depressive symptoms if not for their experiences of less independence in decision-making and lower parent-child closeness. Second, the association between family process and mental health varies by immigrant generation. Low levels of parent-child closeness is not as highly associated with poor mental health among first-generation youth as among youth of other generations. These findings support the hypothesis that family process moderates the association between immigrant generation and mental health. Results indicate that parental education also moderates the association between immigrant generation and depression, and ethnic background moderates the association between immigrant generation and positive affect.

The second question of interest in this chapter is: Does family process help to explain findings of less deviant behavior among first-generation youth compared to other youth? Results indicate that controlling for parental expectations for education, parent-child conflict, and independence in decision-making does reduce the association between immigrant generation and deviant behavior. The reduction, however, is relatively small and the association remains significant. In contrast to findings for depression and positive affect, family process does not significantly moderate the association between immigrant generation and deviant behavior. Rather, sex and ethnicity are the significant moderators in the association between generation status and deviant behavior. The associations between immigrant generation and mental health and behavioral outcomes are discussed in more detail below.

Depressive Symptoms
The results outlined in Chapter 4 indicate a positive association between immigrant generation and depressive symptoms that is explained by sociodemographic factors, particularly household income, parental education, and household size. Family process measures are included in Table 6.1, not to explain the association between immigrant generation and depressive symptoms, but rather to determine if such measures moderate the association. Independence in decision-making, parent-child closeness, and parental involvement are included in equation 2. As stated earlier, these are the family process variables on which first-generation youth, relative to second-generation and third- and higher-generation youth, may be considered disadvantaged given the results outlined in Chapter 5. This disadvantage means that these variables are likely to have more of an effect on the association between immigrant generation and depression.

Results indicate that the addition of independence in decision-making, parent-child closeness, and parental involvement changes the nature of the association in a significant way. First-generation youth, rather than being similar to third- and higher-generation youth as discussed above, now have significantly less depressive symptoms than third- and higher-generation youth. Differences in depression between first- and second-generation and between second- and third- and higher-generation youth remain nonsignificant. Equation 2 also indicates that youth who are highly independent and youth who enjoy a high level of closeness with their parents have less depressive symptoms than youth who are less independent and less close to their parents. Parental involvement is not significantly associated with depressive symptoms. These findings of less depressive symptoms among first-generation youth and youth who experience high independence in decision-making and parent-child closeness indicate

Table 6.1. Depressive Symptoms[a] Regressed on Generation and Family Process

	Equation 1	Equation 2	Equation 3
1st generation[b]	-.025 (.016)	-.030 (.014)*	-.021 (.015)
2nd generation[b]	-.003 (.011)	-.005 (.011)	-.006 (.011)
Age[c]	.016 (.002)***	.012 (.002)***	.012 (.002)***
Age at arrival[d]	.003 (.002)	.002 (.002)	.002 (.002)
Female	.058 (.006)***	.043 (.006)***	.043 (.006)***
Family structure[e]			
Step-parent	.046 (.008)***	.022 (.007)**	.021 (.007)**
One-parent	.048 (.008)***	.045 (.007)***	.045 (.007)***
Other	.061 (.013)***	.044 (.014)**	.044 (.014)**
Household size	.013 (.002)***	.010 (.002)***	.010 (.002)***
Household income[c]	-.016 (.005)**	-.016 (.005)**	-.015 (.005)**
Parents' education[c]	-.009 (.001)***	-.008 (.001)***	-.010 (.001)***
Residence[f]			
Suburb	.013 (.009)	.011 (.009)	.010 (.009)
Rural	.005 (.012)	.004 (.012)	.002 (.012)
Prop. same ethnicity	-.025 (.014)†	-.023 (.013)†	-.021 (.013)
Prop. foreign-born	.063 (.044)	.058 (.041)	.059 (.042)
Prop. poor	.078 (.029)**	.088 (.028)**	.085 (.028)**
Ethnicity[g]			
Mexican	.002 (.013)	.003 (.012)	.005 (.013)
Cuban	-.077 (.036)*	-.076 (.031)*	-.079 (.031)*
Puerto Rican	.028 (.019)	.029 (.021)	.028 (.021)
Other Hispanic	-.027 (.020)	-.025 (.021)	-.027 (.021)
Chinese	.018 (.032)	-.001 (.036)	-.001 (.035)
Filipino	.065 (.024)**	.065 (.024)**	.056 (.024)*
Other Asian	.019 (.021)	.018 (.020)	.013 (.020)
African/Black	.002 (.012)	.005 (.012)	.005 (.012)
Family process			
Independence[c]		-.066 (.015)***	-.067 (.015)***
Closeness[c]		-.140 (.006)***	-.144 (.005)***
Involvement[c]		.001 (.001)	.001 (.001)
Process predicted		.322 (.089)***	.325 (.093)**
Indep. predicted		.097 (.035)**	.100 (.038)**
Interaction			
Closeness x 1st generation			.050 (.020)*
Closeness x 2nd generation			.015 (.018)
Parent education x 1st			.007 (.003)**
Parent education x 2nd			.005 (.003)†
Constant	.628	.648	.655
R²	.072	.156	.157

*** p<.001, ** p<.01, * p<.05, † p<.10 (two-tailed). Unstandardized coefficients (standard errors). [a]Square root adjusts for skewness. [b]Reference category is third and later generations. [c]Measured as mean deviation. [d]Conditionally relevant variable. For the first generation, this variable tests whether the effect of being foreign-born depends on arrival age. [e]Reference category is two-parent. [f]Reference category is urban. [g]Reference category is European/White.

that first-generation youth would have even less depressive symptoms if not for their experiences of less independence in decision-making and lower parent-child closeness.

Equation 3 includes interaction terms to examine the moderating influence of parent-child closeness and parental education on the larger association. Interactions that examine variations in age, sex, income, and ethnic background by immigrant generation are not significant, therefore, are not included in the final model. Figure 6.1 illustrates how the association between parent-child closeness and depression varies by immigrant generation. Depressive symptoms are shown to decrease as parent-child closeness increases across each immigrant generation. At low levels of parent-child closeness, the differences in depression between the immigrant groups are clearly evident with first-generation youth having the lowest level of depressive symptoms and third- and higher-generation having the highest level. The differences between immigrant generations, however, decrease as parent-child closeness increases. At high levels of parent-child closeness, first-generation youth report the highest level of depressive symptoms and third- and higher-generations report the lowest level although the differences are very small.

Figure 6.2 illustrates how the association between parents' education and depression varies with generation. The large difference

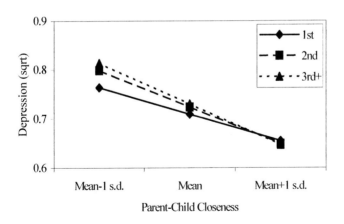

Figure 6.1. Depressive Symptoms by Parent-Child Closeness and Immigrant Generation

in depression between first- and third- and higher-generation youth that
is evident at low levels of parental education is shown to disappear at
high levels of education. Depressive symptoms decrease as parental
education increases for each generation of youth. The decrease is much
more dramatic for third- and higher-generation youth than for youth of
other generations. At low levels of parental education, first-generation
youth are the least depressed and third- and higher-generation youth are
the most depressed. In contrast, at high levels of parental education,
second-generation youth have the highest level of depressive symptoms
with little difference in depression between first-generation and third-
and higher-generation youth. Parental education, thus, has a greater
association with depressive symptoms for third- and higher-generation
youth than it does for first- and second-generation youth.

Overall, foreign-born youth share similar levels of depressive
symptoms with youth of other generations after controlling for
sociodemographic characteristics. Their depression, however, would
be lower if not for their low levels of independence in decision-making,
parent-child closeness, and parental education than youth of other
generations. This supports the hypothesis that family process
moderates the association between immigrant generation and

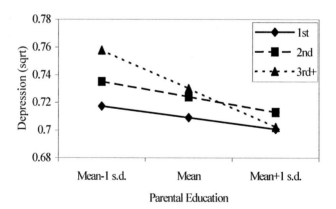

*Figure 6.2. Depressive Symptoms by Parental Education and
Immigrant Generation*

depression; however, support was found for parent-child closeness only.

Positive Affect

In contrast to depressive symptoms, the results of Chapter 4 indicate positive affect increases among higher immigrant generations. This association, however, reduces to nonsignificance after controlling for sociodemographic and community factors, particularly household income, parental education, and household size.

The results from the examination of interaction effects indicate that, as with depression, the association between parent-child closeness and positive affect varies by immigrant generation (Table 6.2). Figure 6.3 shows that at low levels of parent-child closeness, first-generation youth have higher positive affect than both second- and third- and higher-generation youth, who share relatively similar levels. As parent-child closeness increases, however, the positive affect of third- and higher-generation youth increases at a much faster rate than that of other youth, and surpasses the level of positive affect of youth of other generations at high levels of parent-child closeness. The association between parent-child closeness and positive affect, therefore, is greatest for third- and higher-generation youth and lowest for first-generation youth. This finding of a greater association between parent-child closeness and positive affect among third- and higher-generation youth is similar to findings discussed earlier for depressive symptoms.

Results also indicate that the effect of ethnic background on positive affect varies by immigrant generation, something not evident for depression (Figure 6.4). As Cuban is the only ethnic background whose effect significantly varies by immigrant generation, product terms are included that pertain to that background in the final model. The product terms related to other ethnic backgrounds are excluded because they would increase the number of product terms in the final model and increase the probability that a significant interaction effect would be found by chance; thus, Figure 6.4 compares Cubans and Non-Cubans. Several things are noticeable from this graph: (1) first- and second-generation Cubans have greater positive affect than first- and second-generation non-Cubans, and third- and higher-generation Cubans have less positive affect than their non-Cuban counterparts; (2) second-generation Cubans have slightly higher positive affect than first-generation Cubans, and the reverse is true for non-Cubans; and (3) the decrease in positive affect between second-generation and third- and higher-generation youth is much larger among Cubans than among

Table 6.2. Positive Affect Regressed on Generation and Family Process

	Equation 1	Equation 2	Equation 3
1st generation[a]	.039 (.046)	.051 (.045)	.038 (.047)
2nd generation[a]	-.010 (.027)	-.002 (.025)	-.006 (.026)
Age[b]	-.010 (.004)*	-.368e-3 (.005)	-.560e-3 (.005)
Age at arrival[c]	-.009 (.006)	-.006 (.005)	-.008 (.005)
Female	-.065 (.014)***	-.051 (.014)***	-.051 (.014)***
Family structure[d]			
Step-parent	-.078 (.018)***	-.022 (.017)	-.021 (.017)
One-parent	-.047 (.023)*	-.031 (.022)	-.031 (.022)
Other	-.096 (.039)*	-.058 (.041)	-.060 (.041)
Household size	-.023 (.005)***	-.016 (.005)**	-.017 (.005)**
Household income[b]	.040 (.014)**	.033 (.013)*	.032 (.013)*
Parents' education[b]	.029 (.003)***	.024 (.003)***	.024 (.003)***
Education pred	-.143 (.066)*	-.094 (.071)	-.097 (.071)
Residence[e]			
Suburb	-.039 (.022)†	-.033 (.023)	-.034 (.023)
Rural	-.030 (.031)	-.035 (.031)	-.036 (.031)
Prop. same ethnicity	.006 (.029)	.005 (.029)	.002 (.029)
Prop. foreign-born	-.187 (.104)†	-.171 (.099)†	-.178 (.103)†
Prop. poor	-.190 (.074)*	-.185 (.075)*	-.183 (.075)*
Ethnicity[f]			
Mexican	-.078 (.039)*	-.072 (.039)†	-.074 (.039)†
Cuban	.138 (.060)*	.139 (.056)*	-.111 (.121)
Puerto Rican	-.027 (.051)	-.035 (.053)	-.031 (.054)
Other Hispanic	.056 (.054)	.053 (.057)	.059 (.058)
Chinese	-.033 (.068)	.010 (.077)	-.006 (.072)
Filipino	-.193 (.078)*	-.174 (.078)*	-.176 (.080)*
Other Asian	-.104 (.059)†	-.092 (.059)	-.086 (.058)
African/Black	-.011 (.028)	-.016 (.029)	-.017 (.029)
Family process			
Supervision[b]		.167 (.040)***	.169 (.040)***
Closeness[b]		.269 (.014)***	.285 (.014)***
Involvement[b]		.029 (.004)***	.029 (.004)***
Supervision pred		.669 (.264)*	.669 (.262)*
Interaction			
Closeness x 1st generation			-.170 (.047)***
Closeness x 2nd generation			-.082 (.035)*
Cuban x 1st			.276 (.146)†
Cuban x 2nd			.332 (.137)*
Constant	2.212	2.157	2.162
R^2	.052	.123	.124

*** p<.001, ** p<.01, * p<.05, † p<.10 (two-tailed). Unstandardized coefficients (standard errors). [a]Reference category is third and later generations. [b]Measured as mean deviation. [c]Conditionally relevant variable. For the first generation, this variable tests whether the effect of being foreign-born depends on age at arrival. [d]Reference category is two-parent. [e]Reference category is urban. [f]Reference category is European/White.

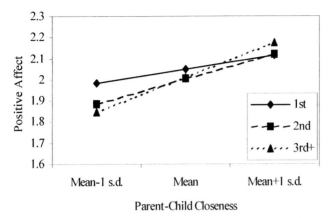

Figure 6.3. Positive Affect by Parent-Child Closeness and Immigrant Generation

non-Cubans. The higher positive affect of first- and second-generation Cubans may be due to them being emboldened by their and their parents' struggle to escape Cuba. Third- and higher-generation Cubans are more removed from such struggle and may be more affected by factors such as perceived discrimination.

Overall, as with depressive symptoms, lower positive affect among foreign-born youth relative to youth of other generations is due to income, parents' education, and household size. Family process does not change the nature of this association. As with depression, however, foreign-born youth appear to function better at lower levels of parent-child closeness than youth of other generations. This supports the hypothesis that family process moderates the association between immigrant generation and positive affect; however, only findings for parent-child closeness are significant.

Deviant Behavior

As outlined in Chapter 4, the results for deviant behavior are very different from those for depression and positive affect with one exception. The lower well-being of second-generation compared to third- and higher-generation youth is explained by sociodemographic factors, namely parents' education. With regard to differences between first-generation youth and youth of other generations, the former report

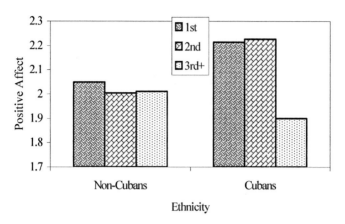

Figure 6.4. Positive Affect by Ethnicity and Immigrant Generation

less, rather than greater, deviant behavior and continue to do so even after controlling for sociodemographic and community factors.

Equation 2 includes controls for parental expectations for education, parent-child conflict, and independence in decision-making. Parental expectations for education and parent-child conflict are being used to help explain deviant behavior because, as stated earlier in this chapter, these are variables on which first-generation youth, relative to second-generation and third- and higher-generation youth, may be considered advantaged given the results outlined in Chapter 5. First-generation youth report higher parental expectations for education and are less likely to report conflict with their parents. This advantage means that these variables are likely to be better at explaining less deviant behavior among first-generation youth than are other measures of family process. Independence in decision-making is included as a control because it is positively correlated with deviant behavior and so may also help to explain the association between immigrant generation and deviant behavior. The addition of controls for parental expectations for education, parent-child conflict, and independence has only a small impact on the association between immigrant generation and deviant behavior. Differences between first-generation and third- and higher-generation youth and between first- and second-generation youth are slightly reduced but remain statistically significant. Equation 2 also indicates that youth who experience high parental expectations

Table 6.3. Deviant Behavior[a] Regressed on Generation and Family Process

	Equation 1	Equation 2	Equation 3
1st generation[b]	-.117 (.028)***	-.090 (.027)**	-.129 (.034)***
2nd generation[b]	.012 (.020)	.019 (.018)	.011 (.021)
Age[c]	.006 (.003)†	.002 (.003)	.002 (.003)
Age at arrival[d]	-.016 (.003)***	-.014 (.003)***	-.014 (.003)***
Female	-.043 (.008)***	-.057 (.008)***	-.061 (.009)***
Family structure[e]			
Step-parent	.053 (.012)***	.045 (.011)***	.045 (.011)***
One-parent	.060 (.012)***	.063 (.011)***	.063 (.011)***
Other	.037 (.020)†	.086 (.019)***	.085 (.019)***
Household size	.003 (.003)	.003 (.003)	.003 (.003)
Household income[c]	.009 (.009)	.012 (.009)	.012 (.009)
Parents' education[c]	.005 (.002)**	.006 (.002)**	.006 (.002)**
Residence[f]			
Suburb	-.012 (.015)	-.017 (.013)	-.017 (.013)
Rural	-.037 (.025)	-.045 (.021)*	-.044 (.021)*
Prop. same ethnicity	-.056 (.023)*	-.037 (.023)	-.037 (.023)
Prop. foreign-born	.103 (.072)	.123 (.055)*	.127 (.055)*
Prop. poor	-.160 (.062)*	-.128 (.054)*	-.130 (.054)*
Ethnicity[g]			
Mexican	.041 (.025)	.039 (.023)†	.042 (.023)†
Cuban	.019 (.050)	.001 (.042)	.004 (.043)
Puerto Rican	.027 (.034)	.025 (.034)	-.027 (.042)
Other Hispanic	.021 (.031)	.023 (.029)	.025 (.030)
Chinese	-.017 (.044)	-.010 (.040)	-.006 (.041)
Filipino	.045 (.038)	.052 (.036)	.055 (.037)
Other Asian	.046 (.038)	.055 (.035)	.060 (.035)†
African/Black	-.047 (.017)**	-.023 (.016)	-.023 (.016)
Family process			
Expectations		-.019 (.006)**	-.019 (.006)**
Conflict		.209 (.009)***	.210 (.009)***
Independence		.110 (.021)***	.111 (.021)***
Process pred, oth		-.101 (.041)*	-.098 (.041)*
Process pred, par		-.279 (.099)**	-.279 (.099)**
Expectations pred		-.454 (.023)***	-.442 (.024)***
Conflict pred		-.285 (.068)***	-.281 (.063)***
Independence pred		-.221 (.100)*	-.219 (.100)*
Interaction			
Female x 1st generation			.070 (.034)*
Female x 2nd generation			-.001 (.026)
Puerto Rican x 1st			.085 (.118)
Puerto Rican x 2nd			.154 (.062)*
Constant	.552	.473	.468
R^2	.031	.099	.100

*** $p<.001$, ** $p<.01$, * $p<.05$, † $p<.10$ (two-tailed). Unstandardized coefficients (standard errors). [a]Square root adjusts for skewness. [b]Reference category is third and later generations. [c]Measured as mean deviation. [d]Conditionally relevant variable. For the first generation, this variable tests whether the effect of being foreign-born depends on arrival age. [e]Reference category is two-parent. [f]Reference category is urban. [g]Reference category is European/White.

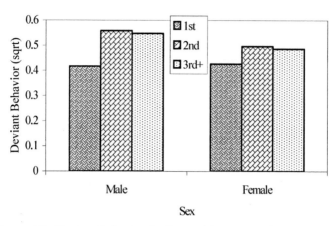

Figure 6.5. Deviant Behavior by Sex and Immigrant Generation

for education, no parent-child conflict, and high independence in decision-making report less deviant behavior than youth who experience low parental expectations for education, some parent-child conflict, and low independence.

The results from tests for interaction effects indicate that the effects of sex and ethnic background on deviant behavior vary by immigrant generation. Figure 6.5 illustrates that females report less deviant behavior than males, with the exception of first-generation youth. First-generation females have slightly more deviant behavior than first-generation males. Additionally, the gap in deviant behavior between first-generation youth and youth of other generations is smaller for females than males. This may signify that females are more negatively affected by the immigration process itself (i.e., the move) and males are more negatively affected by the process of acculturation.

Figure 6.6 illustrates the interaction between ethnic background and immigrant generation for Puerto Rican versus Non-Puerto Rican groups. This comparison is shown because Puerto Rican is the only ethnic background where the effect on deviant behavior significantly varies by immigrant generation. The figure shows that youth of Puerto Rican background report more deviant behavior than non-Puerto Ricans, with the exception of third- and higher-generation youth. Third- and higher-generation youth of Puerto Rican background report less deviant behavior than third- and higher-generation youth of non-

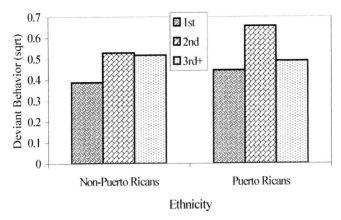

Figure 6.6. Deviant Behavior by Ethnicity and Immigrant Generation

Puerto Rican background. It is also interesting to note the large extent to which second-generation youth of Puerto Rican background experience more deviant behavior than youth of other generations and other ethnic backgrounds.

These results indicate that parental expectations for education, parent-child closeness, and independence in decision-making have only small effects on the association between immigrant generation and deviant behavior. Foreign-born youth continue to report less deviant behavior than youth of other generations even after controlling for sociodemographic and community characteristics as well as family process. This partially supports the hypothesis that family process helps to explain less deviant behavior among foreign-born youth. The differences between foreign-born and other youth are reduced by family process, but not eliminated.

OVERVIEW

This chapter examined the impact of family process on the association between adolescent immigrant generation and depression, positive affect, and deviant behavior. It was expected that family process would affect the larger association between immigrant generation and mental health and behavior because research has shown that factors related to family process may have protective influences on well-being (Patten et al. 1997; Rumbaut 1994a; Dornbusch 1989; Marjoribanks 1987;

Steinberg 1986). Additionally, it had been established in Chapter 5 that adolescent immigrant generations differed on some aspects of family process. The assimilation process may exaggerate differences between parents and youth that may affect family process. Examples of differences include cultural norms where the parents want to maintain tradition and the youth want to adopt the norms of their new society. These differences may lead to intergenerational conflict and such conflict may affect health and behavioral outcomes.

Although the associations between immigrant generation and depression and immigrant generation and positive affect are explained by sociodemographic factors, less deviant behavior among the foreign-born is not. Family process does not entirely explain the differences in deviant behavior between foreign-born and other youth either. The importance of family process is that it has certain aspects, namely parent-child closeness, that moderate the association between immigrant generation and depression as well as positive affect. Low parent-child closeness is not as highly associated with low depressive symptoms and positive affect among the foreign-born as among youth of other immigrant generations. Family process does not appear to moderate the association between immigrant generation and deviant behavior.

Other factors that moderate the association between immigrant generation status and mental health and behavior are parental education, Cuban and Puerto Rican backgrounds, and sex; for example, the depression level of foreign-born youth, compared to youth of other generations, is less affected by their parents' education. These findings may indicate greater maturity and responsibility among foreign-born youth. Surprisingly, adolescent age and household income do not significantly moderate the association between immigrant generation and mental health and behavior.

CHAPTER 7

Physical Health

This chapter focuses on whether family process helps to explain any association between adolescent immigrant generation and physical health outcomes. The focus is on three main measures of physical health: physiological stress response, absence due to illness, and self-rated overall health. As in the previous chapter, the results of analyses from Chapters 4 and 5 are used to frame the analyses.

The high levels of health problems among economically disadvantaged groups and the high likelihood that immigrants are well represented in such groups may lead to the assumption that greater health problems exist among immigrant children. Research findings, however, indicate that immigrant children are likely to be in better physical health than other children (Harris 1999; Hernandez and Charney 1998). The results outlined in Chapter 4 also confirm these findings. Two explanations that have been proposed for these findings are increased exposure to stressors and a reduction in protective factors (Landale et al. 1999). Stressors often relate to language problems, differences in cultural norms, perceived discrimination, and generally unfulfilled expectations. Large differences in cultural norms between parents and children may lead to reductions in protective factors as such differences increase intergenerational conflict and reduce parental authority. Research has found that the beneficial health practices of immigrant families appear to deteriorate as individuals' adherence to cultural norms decrease (Landale et al. 1999). Factors related to family process such as low parent-child conflict and high levels of parent-child closeness have been found to have protective influences on well-being (e.g., Patten et al. 1997; Rumbaut 1994a; Dornbusch 1989); thus, the stresses that immigrant youth encounter during the assimilation process may affect family process and by extension physical health.

Given research findings with regard to the association between immigrant generation and physical health and the association between immigrant generation and family process, it is hypothesized that family process will reduce the association between immigrant generation and physical health.

ANALYTIC STRATEGY
Results from Chapter 4 indicate that foreign-born youth report less physiological response to stress, fewer absences from school due to illness, and greater self-rated overall health than youth of other generations. The results from Chapter 5 indicate that foreign-born youth tend to experience greater parental expectations for education, and less parent-child conflict, parent-child closeness, parental supervision, and parental involvement. Family process measures on which foreign-born youth are found to be at an advantage, relative to other youth, are likely to be better at explaining good health outcomes than family process measures on which they are disadvantaged. Foreign-born youth report better family process than other youth in two respects; namely, greater parental expectations for education and less parent-child conflict. Additionally, family process measures that are significantly and appropriately associated with physical health outcomes are also likely to help to explain the physical health advantage of the foreign-born. As independence in decision-making and parental involvement are positively associated with physiological stress response, these family process measures are tested as possible mediators in the associations between immigrant generation and physiological stress response. The research question is whether or not family process helps to explain less physiological response to stress, fewer school absences due to illness, and better self-rated health of foreign-born youth compared to youth born in the U.S.?

The data is analyzed using regression analyses and the results are displayed in Tables 7.1 to 7.3. These tables may be considered individually or as an extension of Tables 4.4 to 4.6. The first equation in each of the tables in this chapter is the same as the last equation in the equivalent table in Chapter 4. As such, the first equation in Table 7.1 is a duplicate of the last equation in Table 4.4, the first equation in Table 7.2 is a duplicate of the last equation in Table 4.5, and the first equation in Table 7.3 is the same as the last equation in Table 4.6. These equations represent each physical health measure regressed on generation, sociodemographic and community characteristics, and ethnic background. The second equation incorporates the measures of family process. Dummy variables representing imputed/nonimputed family process cases are included in the analyses, but only significant variables are included in the tables to avoid clutter.

Significant product terms are included in the third equation. As in the previous chapter, separate analyses are conducted to determine how the associations between physical health and age, sex, household income, parental education, ethnic background, and family process vary by immigrant generation. Each interaction effect is tested in a separate model. Interactions that are found to be significant are then combined into one model. This unified model is displayed in equation 3.

There is one exception to this approach. Table 7.2, which displays the results for school absence due to illness, consists of four equations. An extra equation is included to control for physiological response to stress prior to the inclusion of interaction terms. This additional control is included because the illnesses that comprise the physiological response index are illnesses that could cause adolescents to be absent from school.

RESULTS

Does family process reduce the association between immigrant generation and physical health? The results are fairly consistent. As with deviant behavior, measures of family process do help to explain the physical health advantage of foreign-born youth relative to youth of other immigrant generations. The significance of family process, however, tends to be small; hence differences between foreign-born youth and other youth remain significant, with one exception. The higher overall health of first-generation relative to second-generation youth is explained by higher parental expectations for education and low parent-child conflict among first-generation youth. This is the only finding related to generation across all health and behavioral outcomes examined that is reduced to nonsignificance after adjusting for family process. As with mental health and behavior, differences in physical health between second-generation and third- and higher-generation youth are not significantly affected by family process as such differences are explained by sociodemographic and community characteristics.

Results indicate that family process, socioeconomic status, and ethnic background moderate the association between immigrant generation and physical health. This is similar to findings for mental health and behavior, except that the particular variables differ. An example of the moderating effects of socioeconomic status is the finding that the physiological stress response of second-generation youth is more strongly associated with household income than that of other youth. In contrast, depressive symptoms are less associated with low parental education among first-generation youth than among other youth as outlined in the previous chapter. The results for physical health are discussed in more detail below.

Physiological Response to Stress
The results outlined in Chapter 4 indicate that first-generation youth have less physiological responses to stress than youth of other immigrant generations even after controlling for sociodemographic and community characteristics. Controlling for parental expectations for education, parent-child conflict, independence in decision-making, and parental involvement result in some decline in the association between immigrant generation and physiological response to stress (Table 7.1). The first-generation coefficient is reduced by 16 percent and the small difference between second-generation and third- and higher-generation youth is eliminated. Equation 2 also indicates that youth who experience high parental expectations for education, no parent-child conflict, low independence in decision-making, and low parental involvement have significantly less physiological response to stress.

Of the interaction effects tested, only the association between household income and physiological response to stress is found to significantly vary by immigrant generation. Figure 7.1 shows that although physiological response to stress increases to varying degrees within each immigrant generation as household income increases, the increase for second-generation youth is much more dramatic than the increase for youth of other immigrant generations. At high levels of income, the physiological response of second-generation youth surpasses that of third- and higher-generation youth. Household income, therefore, has a greater association with the physiological response of second-generation youth than with the response of first- and third- and higher-generation youth. At low levels of income, the physiological response of second-generation youth most closely resembles that of first-generation youth. In contrast, at high levels of

Table 7.1. Physiological Stress Response[a] Regressed on Immigrant Generation and Family Process

	Equation 1	Equation 2	Equation 3
1st generation[b]	-.055 (.016)**	-.046 (.016)**	-.049 (.018)**
2nd generation[b]	-.018 (.009)†	-.015 (.009)	-.018 (.009)†
Age[c]	.315E-3 (.002)	.212E-3 (.002)	.243E-3 (.002)
Age at arrival[d]	-.003 (.002)	-.003 (.002)	-.003 (.002)
Female	.063 (.005)***	.056 (.005)***	.056 (.005)***
Family structure[e]			
Step-parent	.021 (.006)***	.020 (.005)**	.020 (.005)***
One-parent	.024 (.007)**	.027 (.007)***	.027 (.007)***
Other	.020 (.012)†	.036 (.011)**	.036 (.011)**
English in home	.011 (.013)	.008 (.013)	.001 (.013)
Extended family	.009 (.007)	.006 (.007)	.006 (.007)
Household size	.005 (.002)**	.005 (.002)**	.005 (.002)**
Household income[c]	.004 (.005)	.004 (.004)	.001 (.004)
Parents' education[c]	.001 (.001)	.001 (.001)	.001 (.001)
Residence[f]			
Suburb	-.005 (.008)	-.007 (.007)	-.008 (.007)
Rural	-.006 (.009)	-.011 (.008)	-.012 (.008)
Prop. same ethnicity	-.016 (.013)	-.009 (.013)	-.007 (.013)
Prop. foreign-born	-.033 (.032)	-.020 (.026)	-.018 (.026)
Prop. poor	-.035 (.027)	-.019 (.024)	-.019 (.025)
Ethnicity[g]			
Mexican	-.033 (.017)†	-.036 (.017)*	-.033 (.017)†
Cuban	-.022 (.022)	-.032 (.018)†	-.028 (.019)
Puerto Rican	.003 (.018)	-.464E-3 (.018)	.002 (.019)
Other Hispanic	-.042 (.020)*	-.042 (.019)*	-.041 (.019)*
Chinese	.017 (.018)	.020 (.018)	.015 (.018)
Filipino	.008 (.021)	.011 (.021)	.008 (.021)
Other Asian	-.001 (.015)	.741E-3 (.016)	.389E-3 (.016)
African/Black	-.051 (.010)***	-.042 (.010)***	-.043 (.010)***
Family process			
Expectations		-.009 (.003)**	-.009 (.003)**
Conflict		.069 (.004)***	.069 (.004)***
Independence		.030 (.013)*	.030 (.013)*
Involvement		.005 (.001)***	.005 (.001)***
Expectations pred		-.256 (.029)***	-.255 (.029)***
Indep pred		-.568 (.192)**	-.567 (.192)**
Predicted other		-.140 (.024)***	-.131 (.025)***
Interaction			
Income x 1st generation			.007 (.017)
Income x 2nd generation			.030 (.012)*
Constant	.761	.732	.738
R^2	.039	.073	.074

*** p<.001, ** p<.01, * p<.05, † p<.10 (two-tailed test). Unstandardized coefficients with standard errors in brackets. Region is not significant and excluded from table. [a]The square root of this variable is used to adjust for skewness. [b]Reference category is third and later generations. [c]Measured as mean deviation. [d]Conditionally relevant variable. For first generation immigrant youth, these variables test whether the effect of being foreign-born depends on the age at arrival. [e]Reference category is two-parent households. [f]Reference category is urban. [g]Reference category is European/White.

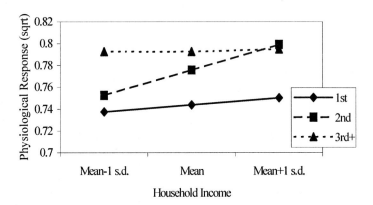

*Figure 7.1. Physiological Stress Response by Household Income and
Immigrant Generation*

income, the physiological response of the second-generation most
resembles that of third- and higher-generation youth.

Although these results indicate that differences between foreign-
born youth and youth of other generations are slightly reduced with the
inclusion of parental expectations for education, parent-child conflict,
independence in decision-making, and parental involvement, the
differences remain significant. Also, the reduction that result from
controlling for sociodemographic and community factors is much
larger than the reduction from further controls for family process
measures. Although the association between immigrant generation and
physiological stress response is reduced and the hypothesis supported,
the association remains significant. It is noteworthy that although
household income is not significantly associated with physiological
response overall, there are important variations by immigrant
generation. Second-generation youth show a dramatic increase in
physiological response at high levels of household income.
This may indicate that the stresses that second-generation youth face at
high levels of income have a greater impact on their health or that
second-generation youth in high income households encounter more
stresses than those in low income households. Second-generation
youth show lower levels of parental expectations for education and
greater likelihood of parent-child conflict than first-generation youth.
With high household income, the cultural gap between what foreign-

born parents want their native-born children to do and what these children themselves want to do may be particularly great.

Absence from School Due to Illness

Statistically significant differences between first-generation youth and youth of other generations are only evident after controlling for sociodemographic and community factors. First-generation youth have fewer absences than other youth. Differences between second-generation and third- and higher-generation youth are generally nonsignificant.

As with physiological stress response, adjusting for family process (in this case, parental expectations for education and parent-child conflict) has little effect on the association between immigrant generation and absences from school due to illness (Table 7.2). The first-generation coefficient shows only a 9 percent decrease and remains statistically significant. The difference between first- and second-generation youth also remains significant. Equation 2 also indicates that youth who experience high parental expectations for education and no parent-child conflict have fewer absences from school due to illness.

There are numerous illnesses that could cause youth to be absent from school. Several of these illnesses are included in the physiological response to stress index. The impact of physiological response on the association between immigrant generation and absences due to illness is outlined in equation 3. Although controlling for physiological response reduces the difference between first-generation and third- and higher-generation youth, the difference remains significant. The difference between first- and second-generation youth, however, is eliminated. Not surprisingly, youth with high physiological response to stress report more absences from school due to illness.

Equation 4 includes interaction terms that examine how the association between immigrant generation and absences varies by parent-child conflict and parental expectations for education. The associations are represented in two illustrations of each interaction. Figures 7.2a and 7.2b illustrate generational variations in the association between parent-child conflict and absences. Youth who experience no conflict have a higher probability of never being absent than those who experience conflict. The probability, however, tends to

Table 7.2. School Absence Due to Illness Regressed on Generation and Family Process

	Equation 1	Equation 2	Equation 3	Equation 4
1st generation[a]	-.453 (.131)**	-.424 (.133)**	-.362 (.128)**	-.329 (.143)*
2nd generation[a]	-.153 (.097)	-.157 (.099)	-.136 (.095)	-.026 (.111)
Generation pred	-.612 (.256)*	-.679 (.319)*	-.825 (.331)*	-.830 (.333)*
Age[b]	.012 (.015)	.009 (.015)	.009 (.015)	.010 (.015)
Age at arrival[c]	-.005 (.021)	-.004 (.022)	-.001 (.024)	-.002 (.023)
Female	.429 (.041)***	.409 (.041)***	.310 (.041)***	.311 (.041)***
Family structure[d]				
Step-parent	.145 (.067)*	.128 (.067)†	.095 (.069)	.097 (.069)
One-parent	.212 (.064)**	.223 (.064)	.164 (.062)**	.163 (.062)**
Other	.330 (.113)**	.335 (.124)**	.273 (.127)*	.274 (.127)*
English in home	.126 (.121)	.102 (.124)	.093 (.121)	.095 (.120)
Extended family	-.098 (.081)	-.093 (.085)	-.101 (.084)	-.098 (.084)
Household size	.031 (.015)*	.030 (.015)*	.016 (.016)	.016 (.016)
Household income[b]	-.105 (.037)**	-.091 (.036)*	-.097 (.039)*	-.096 (.039)*
Parents' education[b]	-.034 (.010)**	-.031 (.010)**	-.033 (.010)**	-.034 (.010)**
Education predicted	.434 (.204)*	.413 (.207)*	.413 (.207)*	.415 (.205)*
Region[e]				
Midwest	-.202 (.072)**	-.191 (.072)**	-.197 (.068)**	-.199 (.068)**
South	-.324 (.079)***	-.305 (.082)***	-.309 (.079)***	-.308 (.079)***
Northeast	-.245 (.095)*	-.227 (.097)*	-.205 (.095)*	-.207 (.095)*

continues on next page

Table 7.2 (cont'd)

	Equation 1	Equation 2	Equation 3	Equation 4
Residence[f]				
Suburb	-.145 (.062)*	-.151 (.063)*	-.152 (.061)*	-.151 (.061)*
Rural	-.290 (.072)***	-.303 (.072)***	-.307 (.070)***	-.307 (.070)***
Prop. same ethnicity	-.151 (.102)	-.119 (.101)	-.114 (.107)	-.114 (.106)
Prop. foreign-born	.268 (.241)	.277 (.240)	.335 (.232)	.302 (.232)
Prop. poor	.751 (.224)**	.753 (.230)**	.776 (.217)***	.763 (.218)**
Prop. predicted	-.599 (.237)*	-.610 (.236)*	-.580 (.250)*	-.588 (.250)*
Ethnicity[g]				
Mexican	-.059 (.101)	-.059 (.103)	-.013 (.101)	-.001 (.101)
Cuban	-.023 (.398)	-.021 (.389)	.044 (.382)	.045 (.380)
Puerto Rican	.160 (.166)	.169 (.166)	.173 (.167)	.173 (.168)
Other Hispanic	-.320 (.169)†	-.301 (.169)†	-.255 (.175)	-.254 (.174)
Chinese	-.394 (.210)†	-.360 (.214)†	-.400 (.221)†	-.389 (.221)†
Filipino	.157 (.215)	.195 (.218)	.186 (.212)	.178 (.210)
Other Asian	-.248 (.175)	-.216 (.179)	-.221 (.182)	-.227 (.180)
African/Black	-.095 (.072)	-.053 (.073)	.012 (.076)	.015 (.076)
Family process				
Expectations		-.086 (.025)**	-.072 (.026)**	-.083 (.028)**
Conflict		.388 (.044)***	.266 (.045)***	.296 (.048)***

continues on next page

Table 7.2 (cont'd)

	Equation 1	Equation 2	Equation 3	Equation 4
Physiological stress response			1.181 (.071)***	1.181 (.071)***
Interactions				
Expectations x 1st generation				.269 (.112)*
Expectations x 2nd generation				-.005 (.082)
Conflict x 1st generation				-.166 (.207)
Conflict x 2nd generation				-.263 (.119)*
Cut points				
1	.780	.943	1.596	1.607
2	3.167	3.342	4.069	4.081
3	4.583	4.761	5.511	5.524
4	5.574	5.752	6.509	6.523
F-statistic	8.82	10.23	15.66	14.24
Degrees of freedom	33, 96	40, 89	41, 88	45, 84

*** $p<.001$, ** $p<.01$, * $p<.05$, † $p<.10$ (two-tailed test)

[a] Reference category is 3rd and later generations
[b] Measured as mean deviation
[c] Conditionally relevant variable
[d] Reference category is two-parent households
[e] Reference category is west
[f] Reference category is urban
[g] Reference category is European/White

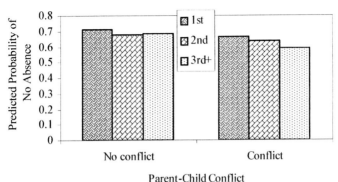

Figure 7.2a. Probability of No Absences by Parent-Child Conflict and Immigrant Generation

decrease in each subsequent generation, with the exception of native-born youth who report no conflict (Figure 7.2a). Among native-born youth who report no conflict, second-generation youth have slightly lower probability of no absences than third- and higher-generation youth. The results for few absences due to illness are presented in Figure 7.2b and are almost the opposite of the findings for no absences.

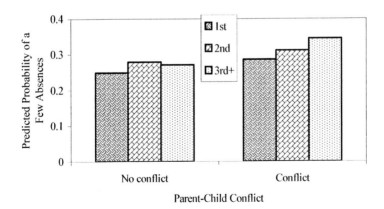

Figure 7.2b. Probability of Few Absences by Parent-Child Conflict and Immigrant Generation

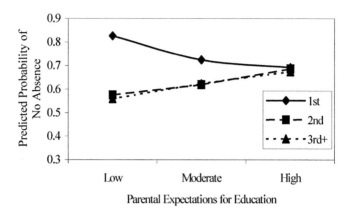

*Figure 7.3a. Probability of No Absences by Expectations for
Education and Immigrant Generation*

The interaction between immigrant generation and parental
expectations for education is illustrated in Figures 7.3a and 7.3b. It is
clearly evident that differences between first-generation youth and
youth of other generations in the probability of being absent due to
illness decrease as parental expectations for education increase.
Although the probability of no absences decreases among first-
generation youth as expectations for education increase, the opposite is
true for second-generation and third- and higher-generation youth—
their probability of absences increases as expectations for education
increase (Figure 7.3a). At higher levels of educational expectations, the
differences in probability between immigrant generations are barely
visible.   Again, Figure 7.3b shows how the association between
immigrant generation and few absences due to illness varies by parental
expectations for education and the results are almost the opposite of
those for respondents who have no absences.

An examination of probability statistics for equation 3 indicates
that first-generation youth have a 70 percent probability of never being
absent compared to only a 3 percent probability of being absent once in
a one-month period.   In contrast, third- and higher-generation youth's
probability of never being absent is 65 percent compared to 4 percent
for one absence.   The probability for second-generation is similar to

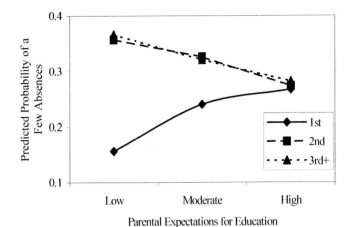

Figure 7.3b. Probability of Few Absences by Expectations for Education and Immigrant Generation

those of the third- and higher-generation with 66 percent and 4 percent probability of zero and one absence, respectively.

These results indicate that controlling for family process leads to some reduction in differences between first-generation youth and youth of other generations, thus supporting the hypothesis. The support, however, is weak as the reduction is small and the differences remain significant. Controlling for physiological response results in a larger reduction in differences among immigrant generations than controlling for measures of family process. The higher physiological response of second-generation youth appears to largely account for the difference in absences between first- and second-generation youth.

Overall Health
As with absences due to illness, differences in overall health between first-generation youth and other youth are only significant after controlling for sociodemographic and community factors. First-generation youth report better overall health than other youth. Second-generation and third- and higher-generation youth report similar levels of overall health.

As with other measures of physical health, controlling for parental expectations for education and parent-child conflict only attenuate the difference between first-generation and third- and higher-generation

Table 7.3. Overall Health[a] Regressed on Generation and Family Process

	Equation 1	Equation 2	Equation 3
1st generation[b]	.042 (.015)**	.037 (.015)**	.055 (.015)***
2nd generation[b]	.013 (.009)	.013 (.009)	.023 (.009)*
Age[c]	-.002 (.001)	-.882E-3 (.001)	-.793E-3 (.001)
Age at arrival[d]	-.315E-3 (.002)	-.519E-3 (.002)	-.687E-3 (.002)
Female	-.039 (.005)***	-.037 (.005)***	-.037 (.005)***
Family structure[e]			
Step-parent	-.027 (.007)***	-.025(.007)**	-.025 (.007)**
One-parent	-.025 (.008)**	-.027 (.008)**	-.027 (.008)**
Other	-.018 (.016)	-.016 (.019)	-.016 (.019)
English in home	-.016 (.015)	-.012 (.015)	-.019 (.014)
Extended family	-.011 (.010)	-.012 (.010)	-.012 (.010)
Household size	-.002 (.002)	-.001 (.002)	-.001 (.002)
Household income[c]	.014 (.006)*	.011 (.006)†	.011 (.006)†
Parents' education[c]	.008 (.001)***	.007 (.001)***	.007 (.001)***
Region[f]			
Midwest	.004 (.009)	.001 (.009)	.001 (.009)
South	.014 (.009)	.011 (.009)	.011 (.009)
Northeast	.023 (.011)*	.021 (.011)†	.020 (.011)†
Residence[g]			
Suburb	-.023 (.007)**	-.023 (.007)**	-.023 (.007)**
Rural	-.022 (.009)*	.021 (.009)*	-.021 (.009)*
Prop. same ethnicity	.009 (.010)	.007 (.010)	.009 (.010)
Prop. foreign-born	-.024 (.028)	-.023 (.028)	-.027 (.028)
Prop. poor	-.125 (.029)***	-.120 (.029)***	-.121 (.029)***
Ethnicity[h]			
Mexican	-.011 (.013)	-.012 (.013)	.012 (.015)
Cuban	.031 (.020)	.031 (.020)	.018 (.020)
Puerto Rican	-.014 (.017)	-.015 (.017)	-.018 (.017)
Other Hispanic	.006 (.019)	.002 (.019)	-.010 (.019)
Chinese	.005 (.023)	.695E-3 (.024)	-.010 (.023)
Filipino	-.048 (.022)*	-.053 (.023)*	-.065 (.022)**
Other Asian	-.037 (.021)†	-.051 (.022)†	-.053 (.021)
African/Black	.038 (.008)***	.034 (.008)***	.034 (.008)***
Family process			
Expectations		.018 (.003)***	.018 (.003)***
Conflict		-.042 (.005)***	-.042 (.005)***
Expectations pred		-.056 (.025)*	-.062 (.025)*
Interaction			
Mexican x 1st generation			-.075 (.034)*
Mexican x 2nd generation			-.049 (.020)*
Constant	2.021	2.036	2.041
R[2]	.039	.050	.050

*** p<.001, ** p<.01, * p<.05, † p<.10 (two-tailed test). Unstandardized coefficients with standard errors in brackets. [a]The square root of this variable is used to adjust for skewness. [b]Reference category is third and later generations. [c]Measured as mean deviation. [d]Conditionally relevant variable. For first generation immigrant youth, these variables test whether the effect of being foreign-born depends on the age at arrival. [e]Reference category is two-parent households. [f]Reference category is west. [g]Reference category is urban. [h]Reference category is European/White.

youth by a small amount (Table 7.3). Further analyses not presented here indicate that adjusting for these measures of family process does reduce the difference in overall health between first- and second-generation youth to nonsignificance. This difference in overall health between first- and second-generation youth is the only difference in the health and behavioral outcomes of immigrant generations examined in this study that is explained by family process. Equation 2 also indicates that youth who experience high parental expectations for education and low parent-child conflict report better overall health. The effect of ethnic background on overall health varies significantly by immigrant generation. As Mexican is the only ethnic background where the effect on overall health significantly varies by immigrant generation, only product terms that pertain to Mexicans are included in the final model. Figure 7.4 compares Mexicans and non-Mexicans. The graph indicates that first- and second-generation youth of Mexican background report worse overall health than first- and second-generation youth of non-Mexican background. Among third- and higher-generation youth, however, Mexicans report better overall health than non-Mexicans. In addition, among youth of Mexican background, third- and higher-generation youth report better overall health than their first- and second-generation counterparts. Figure 7.4 also shows that the gap in overall health between first- and second-generation youth is much larger among non-Mexicans than among Mexicans.

These results indicate that controlling for parental expectations for education and parent-child conflict lead to some reduction in differences between first-generation and youth of other generations. Although the difference between first- and second-generation is reduced to nonsignificance, the difference between first-generation and third- and higher-generation remains significant. Support for the hypothesis of a reduction in differences between first-generation youth and other youth is weak with regard to differences between first-generation and third- and higher-generation, but stronger for differences between first- and second-generation. Findings of an interaction effect for Mexicans indicate that, for the first time in this study, third- and higher-generation youth have a health advantage over first-generation youth. Although Mexicans appear similar to non-Mexicans on other measures of health, first- and second-generation Mexicans perceive themselves to be in poorer health. Among Mexicans, overall health declines among the second-generation, but

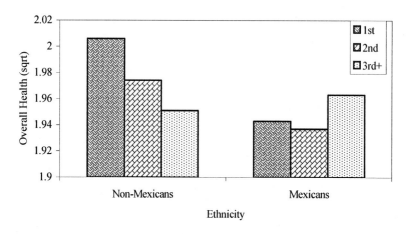

Ethnicity

Figure 7.4. *Overall Health by Ethnicity and Immigrant Generation*
Status

then increases and exceeds the overall health levels of first-generation youth. This seems to indicate that Mexicans experience the same stressors as other second-generation youth as is evident by the decline, but that they recover by the third-generation, whether through increased fortunes or a change in their perception of overall health.

OVERVIEW
This chapter focused on whether measures of family process, specifically parental expectations for education and parent-child conflict, can help to explain better health among foreign-born than native-born youth. It was expected that controlling for family process would reduce differences in physical health between foreign-born youth and youth of other generations because research has shown that factors related to family process may have protective influences on well-being (e.g., Patten 1997; Rumbaut 1994a). Additionally, results of analyses presented in Chapter 5 indicate some generational differences in family process. A frequent source of stress in immigrant families is a gap in cultural norms between parents and children. Such gaps may negatively influence parent-child relationships and family process overall and, by extension, may affect health.

The results indicate some reduction in health differences between foreign-born youth and youth of other generations; however, much of the association remains unexplained. Controlling for measures of family process lead to small reductions in differences between first-generation and third- and higher-generation youth for physiological response to stress, absence due to illness, and overall health. The same is true for differences between first- and second-generation youth, with one exception. Controlling for parental expectations for education and parent-child conflict reduce differences in overall health between first-and second-generation youth to nonsignificance. Hypothesized reductions in health differences between immigrant generations, after controlling for family process, are met, but much of the support is weak. Sociodemographic and community characteristics seem to account for large differences in physiological response between foreign-born youth and native-born youth, and physiological response to stress accounts for large differences in school absences due to illness between foreign-born and native-born youth.

These results further indicate that sociodemographic and community characteristics, including ethnic background, are important factors in explaining differences among immigrant generations. Their importance is also highlighted by findings that the association between immigrant generation and physical health varies by household income and ethnicity. Findings of increasing physiological response among first- and second-generation youth with increasing income and better overall health for third- and higher-generation Mexicans, compared to first-generation, indicate the complexity of the association between immigrant generation and health. Finding explanations for such associations are just as complex; for example, why would third-generation Mexicans be in better overall health than first- and second-generation Mexicans as well as third- and higher-generation non-Mexicans? Is it that Mexicans have some protective influence that is subdued among first- and second-generation youth while they are overwhelmed with the early and mid-stages of the assimilation process, but that is evident in later stages of assimilation? Or is it simply that Mexican youth use a different yardstick when rating their health? The same level of uncertainty exists when trying to explain increases in physiological response at high levels of income, especially among second-generation youth. There are many differences between adolescent immigrant generations, the challenge lies in determining which of these differences will further help to explain the association between immigrant generation and health.

CHAPTER 8

Conclusion

It is evident from this study that the association between immigrant generation and health and behavior is complex. The association between immigrant generation status and particular aspects of health and behavior is often not what would normally be expected. The relationship is also not consistent across outcomes. Further, the role of family process in the association may not be as great as anticipated.

There is a tendency to expect lower well-being among the foreign- than native-born given that the desire to improve economic and social well-being is often a reason for migrating. The results of recent studies have tended to challenge this argument with frequent findings of greater well-being among foreign-born youth and decreasing well-being across subsequent generations (Harker 2001; Harris 1999; Hernandez and Charney 1998; Rumbaut 1994a). Such findings are more supportive of segmented assimilation. The results of this study tend to support those of other studies in this area.

Indications are that foreign-born youth have less physiological stress response, are less likely to be absent from school due to illness, perceive themselves to be in better overall health, and report less deviant behavior than native-born youth after controlling for sociodemographic and community factors. Although differences between foreign-born and native-born youth remain largely unexplained, differences among native-born youth (foreign-born versus native-born parents) are eliminated after adjustments for sociodemographic and community factors. Whereas immigrant youth are becoming more similar to the native-born population, this increasing similarity seems to result in negative consequences. Immigrant youth appear to be on a negative path towards assimilation rather than a positive one. The major change in health and behavior appears to occur between the first- and second-generations.

In contrast to the results for physical health and behavior, foreign-born youth exhibit greater depressive symptoms and lower positive affect than native-born youth. Additionally, among native-born youth, greater depressive symptoms and lower positive affect are found among those youth with foreign-born parents compared to those with native-born parents. Household income, parental education, and household size, however, generally account for these findings. It appears that mental health tends to improve during the assimilation process, but physical health and behavior deteriorates.

Do immigrant generations differ in family process? One of the arguments advanced as an explanation for declining health across generations is intergenerational conflict. Such conflicts often arise because of differences in the acculturation of parents and their children (Zhou 1997; Leslie 1993; Baptiste 1993). Other factors related to family process may also explain deteriorating health, which implies that there are differences in family process across immigrant generations that may relate to acculturative stress.

This study indicates that family process does vary across immigrant generations, but foreign-born youth are not always advantaged. Whereas, foreign-born youth experience greater parental expectations for education and lower parent-child conflict, they also report less independence in decision-making, less parent-child closeness, and less parental involvement than native-born youth. There is no significant association between immigrant generation and social support, as measured in this study. Overall, family process among native-born youth appears to be similar for those with foreign-born and those with native-born parents.

A greater likelihood of conflict and lower parental expectations for education among native-born youth indicate some deterioration in the parent-child relationship and may support the acculturative stress argument that perceived conflicts between new and old cultures may negatively influence parent-child relationships. Whereas low conflict among the foreign-born is largely explained by sociodemographic and community characteristics, higher educational expectations are not. Findings of continued high parental expectations for education among the foreign-born are not surprising given that improved education is a frequent reason for immigrating to the U.S. Additionally, immigrant parents tend to highly encourage educational success in their children (Kao and Tienda 1995). Lower parent-child closeness and lower parental involvement among foreign-born compared to native-born youth are explained by sociodemographic characteristics, but lower independence in decision-making is not.

Although family process (specifically, parental expectations for education and parent-child conflict) does help to explain the association between immigrant generation and deviant behavior, physiological stress response, school absences due to illness, and overall health, the contributions are generally small. Thus, foreign-born youth continue to have better physical health and behavior than native-born youth with native-born parents. Parental expectations for education and parent-child conflict also reduce differences between first- and second-generation youth with regard to deviant behavior and absences from school, and they eliminate significant differences in overall health. Despite the contribution of family process to explaining the physical health and behavior advantage of foreign-born youth, the larger explanation remains unknown.

A surprising finding is the way in which immigrant generational effects on depressive symptoms vary across the analyses. Foreign-born youth, compared to native-born youth with native-born parents, progress from having more depressive symptoms in the bivariate relationship, to having neither more nor less symptoms after controlling for sociodemographic and community characteristics, to having less symptoms after further adjusting for independence in decision-making, parent-child closeness, and parental involvement. This indicates several things. First, foreign birth is related to greater depressive symptoms. Second, sociodemographic factors explain the greater depressive symptoms among immigrant youth. Third, foreign birth has an indirect positive effect on depressive symptoms through family process—the depression of immigrant youth would be even lower if not for their lower levels of independence and parent-child closeness. The results for depressive symptoms also indicate that the depression levels of foreign-born youth, compared to youth of other generations, are less negatively associated with low parent-child closeness and low parental education. Although family process does not significantly change the lack of association between immigrant generation and positive affect, low parent-child closeness has less association with positive affect among foreign-born youth than among native-born youth. These findings may indicate greater maturity and responsibility among foreign-born youth given that they are able to better function in difficult circumstances than other youth.

Significant differences in health and behavior between second-generation and third- and higher-generation youth are explained by sociodemographic characteristics, particularly income and parental education. Further controls for family process have no influence on this relationship.

ADDITIONAL FINDINGS

Several other findings are noteworthy. First, is the general lack of association between age at arrival in the U.S and health outcomes. The argument that age at arrival may impact adaptation is based on the idea that youth who arrived early in childhood are likely to be more similar to native-born youth than are youth who arrived later in childhood (Rumbaut 1994a). Findings from this study, however, indicate that the age at arrival of foreign-born youth is not significantly associated with current health. There is an association with deviant behavior such that foreign-born youth who arrived in the U.S. at a later age report less deviant behavior. Age at arrival also has no association with family process, with the exception of independence in decision-making. Although Rumbaut (1994a) has reported higher depression among more recent arrivals (those living in the country for under 10 years), the effect was weak.

A second noteworthy finding is that the associations between immigrant generation and health and behavior do not vary by adolescent age. Variations in the life experiences of early and late adolescence, thus, do not influence the relationship.

A third finding is that there is little variation in the association between immigrant generation and health and behavior by sex. Not much research attention has focused on sex differences in immigrant advantage. Given that sex differences, however, exist in many aspects of the adolescent experience, there is reason to believe that the associations between immigrant generation and health and behavioral outcomes may vary by sex. Although the results indicate no sex variations in the association between immigrant generation and health outcomes, there is variation in the association between immigrant generation and deviant behavior. Females report less deviant behavior than males, with the exception of first-generation females who report slightly greater deviant behavior than first-generation males. This appears to indicate that the greater deviant behavior exhibited by males is a result of the assimilation process within the U.S.

A fourth finding is that, as with sex, there is little variation in results by ethnic background. This indicates that the experiences of foreign-born youth relative to native-born youth are fairly stable across ethnic groups. Results indicate ethnic background variations in the association between immigrant generation and positive affect, deviant behavior, and overall health. Variations are found for Cubans, Puerto Ricans, and Mexicans, respectively.

SELECTION

Does selection matter? One of the explanations that have been posited for better health and behavior among foreign-born than native-born youth is a selection effect. The argument is that the foreign-born are healthier because they are self-selected from among the healthier population in their native country and simply retain comparatively good health after immigration (Landale et al. 1999; Hernandez and Charney 1998). Although there are merits to this argument, it is very difficult to test in studies such as this one. The pre-migratory characteristics of immigrants that are important in determining the influence of selection are often unavailable. Such characteristics include education level, income, and health status. As the database used for these analyses does not contain such information, the selection argument cannot be adequately tested. There are several reasons, however, to think that selection does not have a large effect on these results.

One reason that these results may not be highly influenced by selection is that they are based on an adolescent sample. It has been argued that selection is less of an issue for immigrant children because they do not generally make the decision to migrate (Landale et al. 1999; Ashworth 1982). Adult relatives usually make migration decisions without input from children. As immigrant children do not make migration decisions, they are not self-selecting out of a population. A counter argument is that if adults with health and socioeconomic advantages decide to migrate, their children are also likely to be advantaged (Gans 1999). An alternative argument is that although child outcomes and parental characteristics are linked, any effects of selection will be less salient for children than for parents themselves. Although adjustments cannot be made for parent and household characteristics prior to immigration in these analyses, adjustments are made for current characteristics.

Selection effects may also be minimized in this study because the results are fairly diverse. Although foreign-born youth have lower mental health than other youth, they tend to report better physical health and behavior than other youth. If selection was a major influence, foreign-born youth should be advantaged in mental health, physical health, and behavior relative to native-born youth. Self-selection from the healthier population should not include individuals with poor mental health.

Selection may also have little effect since a large proportion of immigrants to the U.S. in the past two decades are from Mexico and Latin American countries. Immigrants from such countries represent a broad spectrum of the population of their home countries, not just the affluent or well-educated. Although selection may be relevant for immigrants from countries such as India or Africa entering the country as students, it is doubtful that much of the population from Mexico or Latin America are entering the U.S. in that capacity.

LIMITATIONS
Although this study advances research knowledge on immigrant youth, there are several limitations. One limitation is that the three generations of youth used for comparison purposes were not obtained from longitudinal analysis. Having access to data that follow immigrant youth across three generations, such that the second-generation sample are actually the children of the original group of immigrant youth, and the third-generation sample are the grandchildren of the original group would be ideal. Such data, however, are not available.

Another limitation relates to the measures of family process. Although the five measures of family process used can be considered representative of parent-child relationship and overall family process within a Western cultural context, other measures of family process not examined here may have greater effects on the association between immigrant generation and health and behavioral outcomes. Examples of other measures of family process are parental rules, discipline, supervision, and monitoring. By the same token, the measures employed here may have greater influence on the association between immigrant generation and other health and behavior outcomes not examined here.

An additional limitation relates to the inability to differentiate between refugees and other immigrants in the sample. As the experiences of refugees, both pre- and post-migratory, are likely to be very different from those of non-refugees, examining refugees as a separate group could contribute to a better understanding of adaptation. Their reaction to being in a new country and the effects of the assimilation process may be especially different from that of regular immigrants. Another limitation noted earlier is the lack of data on premigratory circumstances, such as socioeconomic status, health and household composition. Additionally, the study is based on cross-sectional data; thus, determining causation is sometimes an issue.

FUTURE RESEARCH
There are several avenues for further research on the well-being of immigrant youth. One area for future research is to further explain the association between immigrant generation and health and behavioral outcomes. It was anticipated that family process would have a large effect on this association, which it did not. This may have been a function of the measures used.

Other arguments posited as explanations for the health advantage of foreign-born youth should also be examined. An example of one such explanation is perceived discrimination. Although there are difficulties in the operationalization of variables to test this effect, the stress associated with perceived discrimination may be very important for minority youth and could help to explain the deterioration in health and behavior between the first- and second-generations. Another argument relates to cultural differences in norms and beliefs between quickly assimilating children and their more slowly assimilating parents. A third issue worth examining is the influence of peer networks. The individuals with whom immigrant youth socialize, the value they place on such relationships, and the influence of their peers are questions that may yield informative answers. A fourth possible focus is youth activities outside the home such as with schools and other organizations. Such involvement may affect how individuals respond to stressful situations or their vulnerability to stress.

Another suggestion for further research is an examination of other measures of health such as body mass index and more serious illnesses such as asthma and allergies. Body mass index is a measure of obesity, which is a significant public health problem within the United States. The extent to which changes in lifestyle and eating habits that often accompany the assimilation process results in deteriorating health across time and across generations is an important research question. Although some research has been undertaken in this area (e.g., Gordon-

Larsen et al. 2003; Harris 1999), there is still much to be investigated. Asthma and allergies are also of concern. The prevalence of asthma, for example, varies considerably across ethnic groups (Hernandez and Charney 1998) and the small numbers of studies that have examined differences between immigrant generations are contradictory (Harris 1999; Mendoza and Dixon 1999).

Further studies that focus on differences in mental health between immigrant generations are also worthwhile. Research findings for mental health are not as consistent as those for physical health. There are findings of no generational effects as well as findings of positive and negative effects for foreign-born youth. A more detailed examination of various mental health problems and the factors that may result in such diverse findings would make a significant contribution to the field.

Studies that examine common health problems among the U.S. population in addition to common health problems in immigrants' native countries may add considerable insight. Some ethnic groups have been found to exhibit distress in ways different from Americans (Agbayani-Siewert, Takeuchi and Pangan 1999); for example, although depression is a common health diagnosis in the United States, in China, distress is likely to be exhibited through physical pain and fatigue and is likely to be diagnosed as neurasthenia (Kleinman 1986). Findings of low depression among Chinese Americans may lead researchers to conclude that Chinese Americans are in better health than other ethnic groups. An indicator of chronic fatigue, however, may show high levels among Chinese Americans, indicating that they have health problems as well; the problems just differ from those of other ethnic groups.

The results of this study demonstrate that it is sometimes difficult to make large generalizations across immigrant groups. This is especially so for researchers who are interested in explaining differences between various generations of immigrants. What may account for differences in one group may not be a very good predictor for another group; thus, studies that use national databases, but focus on a smaller number of groups may offer more answers than those with greater numbers of groups.

Another area for further research is the extent to which factors that affect the health and behavior of native-born youth are the same for foreign-born youth. For example, findings that low parent-child closeness have less of a negative association with depressive symptoms and positive affect among foreign-born than native-born youth indicate that the protective and risk factors identified for youth in general do not necessarily apply to foreign-born youth to the same extent.

Studies that give greater emphasis to neighborhood effects are also warranted. Community characteristics are mainly used as control variables in this study; therefore, the findings cannot properly address complex neighborhood effects. Such research requires more complex analyses than those employed here, but would test the arguments of segmented assimilation and their application to immigrant youth.

Further studies in the area of immigrant youth would be greatly improved by a national longitudinal study devoted to immigrant adaptation (Hernandez and Charney 1998). The national databases that currently exist fail to provide information on important characteristics, such as reason for immigrating, immigrant status (e.g., refugee, visa), and education and income level prior to leaving the home country. A database that samples immigrants soon after their arrival in a new country would allow for the gathering of such information and would greatly improve the ability of researchers to determine changes in well-being. Such knowledge would also assist in public policy as knowledge on the well-being and life changes of immigrants are generally lacking. Of course, such a large-scale study would be ambitious, but including more questions about immigrant background on existing national longitudinal databases would be an important beginning.

IMPLICATIONS OF FINDINGS
The findings of this study have several implications. One implication is that assimilation into American society is not necessarily a good thing. Findings that show deteriorations in health and behavior across generations clearly imply that not all aspects of the American dream are being realized. The assimilation process is expected to be almost complete by the third-generation (Rumbaut 1997b). Results, however, indicate that third-generation immigrant youth are often in worse health than their foreign-born counterparts.

Another implication is that the foreign-born are not as much of a burden on the U.S. system as is often implied. If foreign-born youth are in better health and engage in less deviant behavior, they are less likely to strain the health (e.g., through repeated use for check-ups and general illnesses) and judicial systems (e.g., through contacts with police). A great deal of attention is focused on the costs of immigrants, such as the resources devoted to English proficiency in schools, but little attention is given to the benefits. Additionally, governments and other decision-makers devote little attention to the loss of such benefits across generations and their potential root causes. In addition to the generally better health and less deviant behavior found in this study, immigrant youth and native-born youth with immigrant parents are also less likely to have engaged in sexual intercourse and to report lifetime usage of three or more substances (Harris 1999). Coupled with these benefits for immigrant youth and children of immigrants generally, however, is the reality that such youth are less likely to have regular access to health care (Capps, Fix and Reardon-Anderson 2003; Klein, Wilson and McNulty 1999). Immigrant youth are also less likely to have health insurance than their native-born counterparts (Capps, Fix and Reardon-Anderson 2003; Lessard and Ku 2003). Additionally, increased overweight among immigrant youth is associated with longer residence in the U.S. (Gordon-Larson et al. 2003). The influence of low wages, poverty, lack of opportunities, and other stresses associated with acculturation is not difficult to envision. A general lack of attention and resources to factors that may derail immigrants during the early stages on their path towards positive adaptation may place future stress on the health and judicial systems. Immigrant youth do not appear to be worse off when they arrive, but they seem to be worse off the longer they stay.

An additional implication relates to findings that depressive symptoms and positive affect are not as negatively associated with risk factors (e.g., low parent-child closeness) among foreign-born as compared to other youth. The implication also relates to findings of better health and behavior among the foreign-born despite their lower levels of independence in decision-making and parental involvement. Such findings imply that some risk and protective factors that relate to health and behavior may be different for foreign-born and native-born youth. This has important clinical implications with regard to mental health. The prevention and treatment of a particular illness among foreign-born and native-born youth should not be identical if the main cause of the illness is different for the two groups. Knowledge of different cultures, thus, may be a prerequisite for successful prevention and treatment of illnesses.

Findings that foreign-born youth may be less affected by low independence and closeness to parents also imply that Western perspectives on family process may not always be appropriate for immigrant families. Different family process should not imply poor family process. The findings also highlight other aspects of the family that may be different for immigrant and nonimmigrant families, such as the presence of extended family members and the experiences of family separation due to migration that are more frequent among immigrant families.

CONCLUSION

Immigrant youth of today have an important role in the future of the United States. Thus, the question of whether foreign-born youth are on an upward or downward path towards assimilation is an important one. The findings of this study are generally inconsistent. Although immigrant youth appear to be on an upward assimilation path with regard to mental health, specifically depression and positive affect, they appear to be on a downward path with regard to behavior and physical health. The assimilation process, thus, appears to be more complex than simply the improvement or deterioration in well-being. Adaptation can lead to improvements in some domains of life and deterioration in others. At the same time that immigrant youth are improving their mental health, they are also reducing their physical health. Although the mental health improvements appear to be due to increases in socioeconomic status, reasons for the decline in physical health are not completely clear given that neither family process, sociodemographic characteristics, or community factors account for the decline.

These findings are also interesting because they are contrary to the usual association between mental and physical health. Mental health and physical health tend to be positively correlated. As indicated above, however, comparisons of immigrant generations indicate that they appear to be operating counter to each other. Thus, among immigrant youth, different factors appear to account for mental and physical health. These are the factors that determine where in society immigrants and their children find themselves—among those who perceive that they have all the opportunities that life in the U.S. has to offer or among those who are disappointed because of their inability to achieve their goals. It is important that we understand why adapting to American society often brings deterioration in health and behavior rather than advancement. This can only be achieved through greater research and the application of such research results to public policy.

Descriptive Statistics for Variables Used in Analysis

Table A.1. Weighted Means, Proportions and Standard Deviations

	Mean	s.d.	Range
Mental Health Outcomes			
Depression	.60	.41	0-2.9
Positive affect	2.02	.68	0-3
Behavior Outcome			
Deviant behavior	.44	.52	0-3
Physical Health Outcomes			
Physiological stress response	.67	.37	0-3.7
School absence due to illness	.41	.64	0-4
Self-rated health	3.87	.91	1-5
Generation Status			
1st generation	.05		
2nd generation	.09		
3rd and over generations	.86		
Age at arrival	8.12	4.72	0-18
English usually spoken at home	.92		
Ethnic Background			
Mexican	.07		
Cuban	.01		
Puerto Rican	.01		
Other Hispanic	.03		
Chinese	.01		
Filipino	.01		
Other Asians	.02		
Black/African background	.16		
White/European background	.68		
Age	15.50	1.82	11-21
Female	.49		
Family Structure			
Two-parent	.55		

continues on next page

Table A.1 (cont'd)

	Mean	s.d.	Range
Step-parent	.16		
One-parent	.23		
Other household	.06		
Extended households	.14		
Household size	4.46	1.57	1-18
Household income	43.77	41.86	2-999
Parents' education	13.57	2.78	0-18
Family Process			
Independence in decision-making	.73	.22	0-1
Parents' educational expectation	4.31	.89	1-5
Parental involvement	4.00	1.96	0-9
Parent-child conflict	.38		0-1
Parent-child closeness	4.43	.58	1-5
Social support	4.01	.60	1-5
Community Characteristics			
West	.17		
Midwest	.31		
South	.39		
Northeast	.14		
Urban	.26		
Suburban	.58		
Rural	.15		
Proportion in poverty	.15	.12	0-.85
Proportion foreign born	.07	.12	0-.87
Proportion same race	.74	.32	

Table A.2. Correlation of Control and Predictor Variables with Immigrant Generation and Family Process

	Generation			Indep.[a]	Expect[a]	Conflict[a]	Close[a]	Involve[a]	Support[a]
	1st	2nd	3rd +						
Depression	.051***	.055***	-.079***	-.041***	-.121***	.199***	-.344***	-.112***	-.426***
Positive affect	-.063***	-.076***	.105***	.068***	.124***	-.089***	.275***	.179***	.332***
Deviant behavior	-.047***	.042***	-.004	.052***	-.042***	.215***	-.227***	-.047***	-.309***
Physiol. response	-.054***	-.019**	.052***	.026***	-.045***	.161***	-.163***	.054***	-.205***
School absence	-.009	.007	-.2E-3	.008	-.060***	.085***	-.087***	.004	-.104***
Overall health	.006	-.027***	.019*	.004	.096***	-.079***	.171***	.115***	.220***
Age at arrival	.040***	-.005	-.023**	-.031***	-.003	-.010	-.013†	-.006	.011
English at home	-.563***	-.330***	.647***	.066***	-.008	.019**	.034***	.050***	-.016*
Mexican	.111***	.283***	-.308***	-.055***	-.056***	.013†	-.049***	-.033***	-.013†
Cuban	.224***	.175***	-.294***	.017*	.016*	-.020**	.003	-.021**	.019**
Puerto Rican	-.004	.103***	-.083***	.001	.010	.018	.010	-.001	-.002
Other Hispanic	.233***	.073***	-.215***	-.022**	.015*	.001	-.009	-.008	-.002
Chinese	.136***	.135***	-.202***	.002	.040***	-.003	-.013†	-.019**	-.009
Filipino	.283***	.143***	-.307***	-.004	.038***	2E-3	-.031***	-.032***	-.006
Other Asians	.154***	.137***	-.215***	-.021**	.027***	-.003	-.011	-.015*	-.011
African/Black	-.113***	-.140***	.191***	-.051***	.011	-.057***	.029***	-.024**	-.001

continues on next page

Table A.2 (cont'd)

	Generation			Indep.[a]	Expect[a]	Conflict[a]	Close[a]	Involve[a]	Support[a]
	1st	2nd	3rd +						
European	-.291***	-.277***	.423***	.081***	-.023**	.037***	.022**	.071***	.020**
Age	.135***	.044***	-.126***	.317***	-.055***	.003	-.150***	-.097***	-.167***
Female	-.005	-.012†	.013†	.004	.020**	.060***	-.095***	.102***	.014†
Two-parent	.025***	.128***	-.122***	-.033***	.065***	.014†	.057***	.128***	.101***
Step-parent	-.032***	-.078***	.086***	.001	-.039***	.037***	-.112***	-.023**	-.062***
One-parent	-.025***	-.069***	.074***	.028***	-.015*	-.026***	.040***	-.108***	-.036***
Other household	.045***	-.025***	-.010	.019**	-.056***	-.046***	-.024**	-.043***	-.050***
Extended family	.083***	.041***	-.089***	.001	-.037***	-.029***	-.013†	-.053***	-.028***
Household size	.115***	.109***	-.167***	-.099***	-.035***	.001	-.053***	-.013†	.002
Household income	-.146***	-.011	.105***	.065***	.124***	.023***	.016*	.159***	.044***
Parent education	-.139***	-.120***	.191***	.059***	.171***	.027***	.039***	.181***	.040***
Independence	-.037***	-.030***	.049***	1.000	—	—	—	—	—
Expectation	.035***	.020**	-.040***	-.017*	1.000	—	—	—	—
Conflict	-.024**	.008	.009	-.016*	.019**	1.000	—	—	—
Closeness	-.041***	-.024**	.046***	-.047***	.139***	-.195***	1.000	—	—

continues on next page

Table A.2 (cont'd)

	Generation			Indep.[a]	Expect[a]	Conflict[a]	Close[a]	Involve[a]	Support[a]
	1st	2nd	3rd +						
Involvement	-.048***	-.026***	.053***	-.038***	.136***	.122***	.284***	1.000	—
Social support	.009	-.009	.002	-.076***	.135***	-.213***	.622***	.277***	1.000
West	.138***	.182***	-.243***	-.013†	-.019**	-.016*	-.061***	-.011	-.052***
Midwest	-.132***	-.117***	.184***	.053***	.002	.022**	-.017*	.014†	-.026***
South	-.011	-.086***	.079***	-.062***	-.005	-.043***	.061***	.008	.060***
Northeast	.005	.037***	-.034***	.037***	.027***	.012	.012	-.014†	.012†
Urban	.110***	.108***	-.162***	-.029***	.048***	-.010	.023**	.001	.032***
Suburban	-.010	.002	.005	.009	.002	.008	-.017*	-.011	-.031***
Rural	-.122***	-.135***	.193***	.023**	-.061***	.002	-.004	.014†	.002
Proportion poor	.035***	-.045***	.014†	-.088***	-.060***	-.053***	.030***	-.078***	.013†
Prop. foreign born	.448***	.358***	-.594***	-.017*	.026***	-.019*	-.041***	-.060***	-.001
Prop. same race	-.213***	-.252***	.351***	.058***	-.031***	-.004	.029***	.042***	.034***

*** $p<.001$, ** $p<.01$, * $p<.05$, † $p<.10$ (two-tailed test)

[a]Indep. = Independence in decision-making
Expect = Parental expectations for education
Conflict = Parent-child conflict
Close = Parent-child closeness
Involve = Parental involvement
Support = Social Support

Table A.3. Weighted Means and Proportions by Immigrant Generation

	1st	2nd	3rd +
Mental health outcomes			
Depression	.68*	.63*	.59*
Positive affect	1.84*	1.92*	2.04*
Behavior outcome			
Deviant behavior	.33*	.49*	.44*
Physical health outcomes			
Physiological stress response	.59*	.64*	.68*
School absence due to illness	.36	.39	.41
Overall health	3.89	3.88	3.88
English spoken at home	.27***	.65***	.99***
Ethnic background			
Mexican	.27	.28	.03***
Cuban	.04	.05	.12E-2
Puerto Rican	.02	.05*	.01
Other Hispanic	.21**	.08**	.01**
Chinese	.05	.03	.20E-2**
Filipino	.11	.05	.19E-2*
Other Asian	.18**	.07**	.39E-2**
Black/African background	.05	.06	.18
White/European background	.07***	.32***	.76***
Age	16.02**	15.50	15.44
Female	.51	.47	.49
Family structure			
Two-parent household	.58	.73***	.53
Step-parent household	.12*	.09*	.17*
One-parent household	.21	.15**	.25
Other household	.09**	.03	.05
Extended household	.22*	.16	.13
Household size	5.26*	5.03*	4.37*
Household income	29.14***	44.43	46.22
Parents' education	11.59***	12.78***	13.80***

continues on next page

137

Table A.3 (cont'd)

	1st	2nd	$3^{rd}+$
Parent-child association			
Independence	.68	.70	.74**
Educational expectation	4.43*	4.31	4.31
Parent-child closeness	4.36**	4.42	4.44**
Parent-child conflict	.32**	.39	.38
Parental involvement	3.70**	3.89	4.04**
Social support	4.04	4.03	4.01
Community characteristics			
West	.34	.30	.14*
Midwest	.07**	.17**	.34**
South	.38	.32	.39
Northeast	.21	.21*	.13*
Urban	.57	.47	.22***
Suburban	.42	.47*	.60*
Rural	.01*	.05*	.17*
Proportion same race	.39**	.51**	.79**
Proportion foreign-born	.29**	.18**	.04**
Proportion in poverty	.18*	.14*	.14

*** $p<.001$, ** $p<.01$, * $p<.05$

Interpretation of *: - If only one number in a particular row (excluding total column) contains an asterisk then that number is significantly different from the other two. If two numbers in a particular row contain asterisks then the two numbers are significantly different from each other. If all three numbers in a particular row contain asterisks then the three numbers are significantly different from each other.

Table A.4. Weighted Means of Family Process and Well-Being Measures by Ethnicity and Immigrant Generation

	Mexican			Puerto Rican			Cuban		
	1st	2nd	3rd+	1st	2nd	3rd+	1st	2nd	3rd+
Outcomes									
Depression	.74*	.72	.64*	.60	.71	.69	.60*	.53*	.75
Positive affect	1.64	1.70	1.95***	2.19*	1.83*	1.92	2.04	2.02	1.71*
Deviant behavior	.29****	.50	.55	.55	.66	.51	.29****	.54***	.50
Physiol. response	.57**	.63	.68**	.73	.72	.66	.45***	.62	.73
Sick days	.42	.45	.50	.45	.60	.55	.42	.41	.57
Overall health	3.66	3.69*	3.83*	3.59	3.76	3.80	4.02	3.91	4.04
Family process									
Independence	.64	.65	.73**	.53**	.71	.75	.80	.67	.78
Expectation	4.17	4.12	4.16	4.53	4.33	4.24	4.49***	4.22***	3.95
Closeness	4.25*	4.36	4.43	4.69***	4.50	4.41***	4.53	4.44	4.08*
Conflict	.28**	.43	.43	.55*	.35*	.46	.33	.32	.39
Involvement	3.47*	3.79	3.93*	4.89**	3.98	3.69**	3.75***	3.24***	3.33
Social support	4.07	3.99	4.02	3.97	4.08	3.99	4.01	4.16	3.79
N	281	700	586	38	173	302	224	244	34

continues on next page

Table A.4 (cont'd)

	Other Hispanic			Chinese			Filipino		
	1st	2nd	3rd+	1st	2nd	3rd+	1st	2nd	3rd+
Outcomes									
Depression	.66	.70	.57	.66	.56	.63	.71	.72	.67
Positive affect	1.93	1.93	2.06	1.94	2.07	2.07	1.89	1.75	1.88
Deviant behavior	.27**	.49	.57	.42	.44	.49	.46	.55	.50
Physiol. response	.56*	.60	.67*	.69	.62	.69	.67	.64	.73
Sick days	.40*	.25*	.37	.22	.23	.39	.37	.38	.75*
Overall health	4.04	3.79	3.83	4.05	3.98	4.00	3.97**	3.56**	3.71
Family process									
Independence	.66	.69	.76	.73	.77	.67	.71	.73	.72
Expectation	4.49*	4.24*	4.38	4.42	4.65	4.57	4.53	4.56	4.42
Closeness	4.44	4.38	4.38	4.14	4.27	4.59**	4.30	4.35	4.47
Conflict	.29	.39	.36	.37	.39	.27	.38	.36	.35
Involvement	3.87	3.84	3.86	3.73	3.80	4.35	3.86	3.59	3.69
Social support	4.10*	4.07	3.89*	3.77*	4.01	4.18*	4.07	3.89*	4.15
N	228	138	125	121	160	66	294	231	50

continues on next page

Table A.4 (cont'd)

	Other Asian			African/Black			European/White		
	1st	2nd	3rd+	1st	2nd	3rd+	1st	2nd	3rd+
Outcomes									
Depression	.68	.54*	.69	.61	.63	.66	.55	.55	.57
Positive affect	1.81*	2.04*	1.79	1.86	1.97	1.95	2.02	2.10	2.07
Deviant behavior	.37*	.63*	.51	.24	.37	.37	.35	.44	.45
Physiol. response	.61*	.63	.71*	.46*	.60	.65	.57*	.66	.69
Sick days	.22	.35	.41	.45	.36	.45	.30	.36	.39
Overall health	3.78	3.96*	3.66*	4.21***	4.07	3.87***	4.07	4.08***	3.88***
Family process									
Independence	.71	.72	.73	.69	.68	.72	.71	.74	.74
Expectation	4.52	4.54	4.49	4.54	4.26	4.27	4.75***	4.38	4.32
Closeness	4.42	4.48	4.32	4.28	4.39	4.46	4.51	4.47	4.44
Conflict	.35	.41	.31	.13**	.34	.32	.36	.37	.39
Involvement	3.64	4.21	4.32	2.68*	3.44	3.76	4.33	4.14	4.11
Social support	3.97	4.01	3.86	4.03	4.03	3.99	4.11	4.05	4.01
N	158	194	109	87	166	3796	62	437	9667

*** $p < .001$, ** $p < .01$, * $p < .05$. <u>Interpretation:</u> - If only one number in a particular row for each ethnic background contains an asterisk then that number is significantly different from the other two. If two numbers in a particular row for each ethnicity contain asterisks then the two numbers are significantly different from each other. If all three numbers in a particular row for each ethnicity contain asterisks then the three numbers are significantly different from each other.

Notes

1. Sampling information in this section was obtained from (Chantala and Tabor 1999; Tourangeau and Shin 1998; Bearman, Jones, and Udry 1997).

2. For detailed information on Add Health's weighting procedures, please consult (Tourangeau and Shin 1998).

3. http://www.cpc.unc.edu/projects/addhealth/faq/8.html, July 6, 1999.

4. Discriminant analysis uses cases that have already been classified as either second- or third- and higher-generation to derive mathematical equations. These equations allow for the identification of the group to which a particular case has the highest probability of belonging (Klecka 1980). The equations used for classification are considered good. A crosstab of observed and predicted cases indicates 92 percent accuracy in classification.

5. The discriminant function has an accuracy rate of 67 percent for observed and predicted cases.

References

Agbayani-Siewert, Pauline, David Takeuchi, and Rosavinia Pangan. 1999.
"Mental Illness in a Multicultural Context." Pp. 19-36 in *Handbook of the Sociology of Mental Health*, edited by C. Aneshensel and J. Phelan. New York: Plenum.

Aiken, Leona S. and Stephen G. West. 1991. *Multiple Regression: Testing and Interpreting Interactions*. Newbury Park, CA: Sage.

Alba, Richard D. 1985. *Italian Americans: Into the Twilight of Ethnicity*. Englewood Cliffs, NJ: Prentice-Hall.

American Psychiatric Association. 1994. *Diagnostic and Statistical Manual of Mental Disorders*. 4th ed. Washington, DC: American Psychiatric Association.

Aneshensel, Carol S. and Clea A. Sucoff. 1996. "The Neighborhood Context of Adolescent Mental Health." *Journal of Health and Social Behavior* 37:293-310.

Ashworth, M. 1982. "The Cultural Adjustment of Immigrant Children in English Canada." Pp. 77-83 in *Uprooting and Surviving*, edited by R. C. Nann. Boston, MA: D. Reidel.

Baumol, William J., Alan S. Blinder, and William M. Scarth. 1988. *Economics Principles and Policy*. 2d ed. Toronto, ON: Harcourt, Brace, Jovanovich.

Baptiste, David A. 1993. "Immigrant Families, Adolescents, and Acculturation: Insights for Therapists." *Marriage and Family Review* 19:341-63.

Barlow, Sarah E. and William H. Dietz. 1998. "Obesity Evaluation and Treatment: Expert Committee Recommendations." *Pediatrics* 102(3):e29.

145

Baydar, Nazli. 1988. "Effects of Parental Separation and Reentry into Union on the Emotional Well-Being of Children." *Journal of Marriage and the Family* 50:967-81.

Bearman, Peter S., Jones, Jo, and Udry, J. Richard. 1997. "The National Longitudinal Study of Adolescent Health: Research Design" [Web Page]. Accessed 1 Jun 1998. Available at http://www.cpc.unc.edu/projects/addhealth/design.html.

Beiser, Morton, Feng Hou, Ilene Hyman and Michel Tousignant. 2002. "Poverty, Family Process, and the Mental Health of Immigrant Children in Canada." *American Journal of Public Health* 92:220-26.

Berk, Richard A. 1983. "Applications of the General Linear Model to Survey Data." Pp. 495-546 in *Handbook of Survey Research*, edited by P. H. Rossi, J. D. Wright, and A. B. Anderson. San Diego, CA: Academic Press.

Berry, John W. 1970. "Marginality, Stress, and Ethnic Identification in an Acculturated Aboriginal Community." *Journal of Cross-Cultural Psychology* 1:239-52.

Berry, John W. 1980. "Acculturation as Varieties of Adaptation." Pp. 9-25 in *Acculturation: Theory, Models and Some New Findings*, edited by A. Padilla. Boulder CO: Westview.

Billy, John O. G., Audra T. Wenzlow, and William R. Grady. 1998. "National Longitudinal Study of Adolescent Health: Part I--Wave I and II Contextual Database." Chapel Hill, NC: Carolina Population Center, University of North Carolina at Chapel Hill.

Blake, Judith. 1981. "Family Size and the Quality of Children." *Demography* 18:421-42.

Boyce, Thomas. 1985. "Social Support, Family Relations, and Children." *Social Support and Health*, edited by S. Cohen and S. L. Syme. New York: Academic Press.

Brindis, Claire, Amy L. Wolfe, Virginia McCarter, Shelly Ball, and Susan Starbuck-Morales. 1995. "The Association Between Immigrant Status and Risk-Behavior Patterns in Latino Adolescents." *Journal of Adolescent Health* 17:99-105.

Buriel, Raymond and Terri De Ment. 1997. "Immigration and Sociocultural Change in Mexican, Chinese, and Vietnamese American Families." Pp. 165-200 in *Immigration and the Family: Research and Policy on U.S. Immigrants*, edited by A. Booth, A. C. Crouter, and N. Landale. Mahwah, NJ: Lawrence Erlbaum Associates.

Burnam, M. Audrey, Richard Hough, Marvin Karno, Javier I. Escobar, and Cynthia A. Telles. 1987. "Acculturation and Lifetime Prevalence of Psychiatric Disorders Among Mexican Americans in Los Angeles." *Journal of Health and Social Behavior* 28:89-102.

Bush, Kevin Ray. 2000. "Separatedness and Connectedness in the Parent-Adolescent Relationship as Predictors of Adolescent Self-Esteem in US and Chinese Samples." *Marriage and Family Review* 30:153-78.

Cabral, Howard, Lise E. Friend, Suzette Levenson, Hortensia Amaro, and Barry Zuckerman. 1990. "Foreign-Born and US-Born Black Women: Differences in Health Behaviors and Birth Outcomes." *American Journal of Public Health* 80:70-72.

Cannon, Walter B. 1932. *The Wisdom of the Body*. New York: W.W. Norton & Co., Inc.

Capps, Randy, Michael Fix and Jane Reardon-Anderson. 2003. "Children of Immigrants Show Slight Reductions in Poverty, Hardship." *Snapshots of America's Families 3, No. 13)*. Washington, DC: The Urban Institute.

Carolina Population Center. 1999. [Web Page]. Accessed 6 Jul 1999. Available at http://www.cpc.unc.edu/projects/addhealth/faq/8.html.

Chantala, Kim and Joyce Tabor. 1999. "Strategies to Perform a Design-Based Analysis Using the Add Health Data." Chapel Hill, NC: Carolina Population Center, University of North Carolina at Chapel Hill.

Child, Irving L. 1943. *Italian or American? The Second Generation in Conflict*. New Haven, CT: Yale University Press.

Chiswick, Barry R. 1977. "Sons of Immigrants: Are They at an Earnings Disadvantage?" *American Economic Review* 67:376-80.

Chiu, Lian-hwang. 1987. "Child-Rearing Attitudes of Chinese, Chinese-American, and Anglo-American Mothers." *International Journal of Psychology* 22:409-19.

Chiu, Martha Li, S. Shirley Feldman, and Doreen A. Rosenthal. 1992. "The Influence of Immigration on Parental Behavior and Adolescent Distress in Chinese Families Residing in Two Western Nations." *Journal of Research on Adolescence* 2:205-39.

CIA. 2000. "The World Factbook" [Web Page]. Accessed 19 Sep 2001. Available at http://www.odci.gov/cia/publications/factbook/docs/notes.html.

Cohen, Jacob. 1968. "Multiple Regression As a General Data-Analytic System." *Psychological Bulletin* 70:426-43.

Cohen, Jacob and Patricia Cohen. 1983. *Applied Multiple Regression/Correlation Analysis for the Behavioral Sciences*. 2d ed. Hillsdale, NJ: Lawrence Erlbaum.

Cohen, Sheldon and S. Leonard Syme. 1985. "Issues in the Study and Application of Social Support." Pp. 3-12 in *Social Support and Health*, edited by S. Cohen and S. L. Syme. New York: Academic Press.

Coll, Cynthia G. and Katherine Magnuson. 1997. "The Psychological Experience of Immigration: A Development Perspective." Pp. 91-131 in *Immigration and the Family: Research and Policy on U.S. Immigrants*, edited by A. Booth, A. C. Crouter, and N. Landale. Mahwah, NJ: Lawrence Erlbaum Associates.

Collins, W. Andrew and Coral Luebker. 1994. "Parent and Adolescent Expectancies: Individual and Relational Significance." Pp. 65-80 in *Beliefs About Parenting: Origins and Developmental Implications*, edited by J. G. Smetana. San Francisco, CA: Jossey-Bass.

Collins, James W. Jr. and David K. Shay. 1994. "Prevalence of Low Birth Weight Among Hispanic Infants With United States-Born and Foreign-Born Mothers: The Effect of Urban Poverty." *American Journal of Epidemiology* 139:184-92.

Cropley, A. J. 1983. *The Education of Immigrant Children: A Social-Psychological Introduction*. London: Croom Helm.

Crockett, Lisa J. and Ann C. Crouter. 1995. "Pathways Through Adolescence: An Overview." Pp. 1-14 in *Pathways Through Adolescence: Individual Development in Relation to Social Contexts*, edited by L. J. Crockett and A. C. Crouter. Mahwah, NJ: Lawrence Erlbaum Associates.

Davies, Allyson R. and John E. Ware. 1981. *Measuring Health Perceptions in the Health Insurance Experiment* . Santa Monica, CA: Rand Corporation. R-2711-HHS.

Dornbusch, Sanford M., Phillip L. Ritter, P. Herbert Leiderman, Donald F. Roberts, and Michael J. Fraleigh. 1987. "The Relation of Parenting Style to Adolescent School Performance." *Child Development* 58:1244-57.

Dornbusch, Sanford M. 1989. "The Sociology of Adolescence." *Annual Review of Sociology* 15:233-59.

Dornbusch, Sanford M., J. Merrill Carlsmith, Steven J. Bushwall, Phillip L. Ritter, Herbert Leiderman, Albert H. Hastorf and Ruth T. Gross. 1985. "Single Parents, Extended Households, and the Control of Adolescents." *Child Development* 56:326-41.

Dublin, Thomas 1996. *Becoming American, Becoming Ethnic: College Students Explore Their Roots*. Philadelphia, PA: Temple University Press.

Echechipia, S., P. Ventas, M. Audicana, I. Urrutia, G. Gastaminza, F. Polo, and L. Fernandez de Corres. 1995. "Quantitation of Major Allergens in Dust Samples From Urban Populations Collected in Different Seasons in Two Climatic Areas of the Basque Region (Spain)." *Allergy* 50:478-82.

Feldman, S. Shirley and Doreen A. Rosenthal. 1990. "The Acculturation of Autonomy Expectations in Chinese Highschoolers Residing in Two Western Nations." *International Journal of Psychology* 25:259-81.

Field, Tiffany, Claudia Lang, Regina Yando, and Debra Bendell. 1995. "Adolescents' Intimacy With Parents and Friends." *Adolescence* 30:133-40.

Fix, Michael E. and Jeffrey A. Passel. 2003. "U.S. Immigration: Trends and Implications for Schools". National Association for Bilingual Education, New Orleans, LA, January 28th. Washington, DC: The Urban Institute. http://www.urban.org/url.cfm?ID=410654.

Fox, Jeanne, Elizabeth Merwin, and Michael Blank. 1995. "De Facto Mental Health Services in the Rural South." *Journal of Health Care for the Poor and Underserved* 6:434-69.

Fuligni, Andrew. 1997. "The Academic Achievement of Adolescents from Immigrant Families: The Roles of Family Background, Attitudes, and Behavior." *Child Development* 68:351-63.

Gans, Herbert J. 1992. "Second-Generation Decline: Scenarios for the Economic and Ethnic Future of the Post-1965 American Immigrants." *Ethnic and Racial Studies* 15:173-92.

———. 1999. "Filling in Some Holes: Six Areas of Needed Immigration Research." *American Behavioral Scientist* 42:1302-13.

Gibson, Margaret A. and John U. Ogbu. 1991. *Minority Status and Schooling: A Comparative Study of Immigrant and Involuntary Minorities*. New York: Garland Publishing, Inc.

Gil, Andres G. and William A. Vega. 1996. "Two Different Worlds: Acculturation Stress and Adaptation Among Cuban and Nicaraguan Families." *Journal of Social and Personal Relationships* 13:435-56.

Gil, Andres G., William A. Vega, and Dimas Juanita M. 1994. "Acculturative Stress and Personal Adjustment Among Hispanic Adolescent Boys." *Journal of Community Psychology* 22:43-55.

Gordon, Milton M. 1964. *Assimilation in American Life: The Role of Race, Religion, and National Origins*. New York: Oxford University Press.

Gordon-Larsen, Penny, Kathleen Mullan Harris, Dianne S. Ward, and Barry M. Popkin. 2003. "Acculturation and Overweight-Related Behaviors Among Hispanic Immigrants to the US: The National Longitudinal Study of Adolescent Health". *Social Science and Medicine* 57:2023-34.

Gore, Susan, Robert H. Aseltine, and Mary E. Colton. 1992. "Social Structure, Life Stress and Depressive Symptoms in a High School-Aged Population." *Journal of Health and Social Behavior* 33:97-113.

Greeley, Andrew M. 1976. "The Ethnic Miracle." *Public Interest* 45:20-36.

Greenberg, Mark T., Judith M. Siegel, and Cynthia J. Leitch. 1983. "The Nature and Importance of Attachment Relationships to Parents and Peers During Adolescence." *Journal of Youth and Adolescence* 12:373-86.

Guendelman, Silvia and Barbara Abrams. 1995. "Dietary Intake Among Mexican American Women: Generational Differences and a Comparison With White Non-Hispanic Women." *American Journal of Public Health* 85:20-25.

Guendelman, Silvia, Paul English, and Gilberto Chavez. 1995. "Infants of Mexican Immigrants: Health Status of an Emerging Population." *Medical Care* 33:41-52.

Guendelman, Silvia and Paul B. English. 1995. "Effects of United States Residence on Birth Outcomes Among Mexican Immigrants: An Exploratory Study." *American Journal of Epidemiology* 142:S30-S38.

Guo, Shumei. S., Alex F. Roche, W. Cameron Chumlea, Jane D. Gardner, and Roger M. Siervogel. 1994. "The Predictive Value of Childhood Body Mass Index Values for Overweight at Age 35 Years." *American Journal of Clinical Nutrition* 59:810-819.

Hamilton, Lawrence C. 1992. *Regression With Graphics: A Second Course in Applied Statistics*. Pacific Grove, CA: Brooks/Cole.

Handlin, Oscar. 1951. *The Uprooted: The Epic Story of the Great Migrations That Made the American People*. Boston: Little, Brown.

Harker, Kathryn. 2001. "Immigrant Generation, Assimilation, and Adolescent Psychological Well-Being." *Social Forces* 79:969-1004.

Harris, Kathleen M. 1999. "Health Status and Risk Behaviors of Adolescents in Immigrant Families." Pp. 286-347 in *Children of Immigrants: Health, Adjustment, and Public Assistance*, edited by D. J. Hernandez, Committee on the Health and Adjustment of Immigrant Children and Families, and Board on Children, Youth and Families. Washington, DC: National Academy Press.

Hernandez, Donald. 2004. "Demographic Change and the Life Circumstances of Immigrant Families." *The Future of Children* 14(2):17-47.

Hernandez, Donald J. and Evan Charney, ed. 1998. *From Generation to Generation: The Health and Well-Being of Children in Immigrant Families*. Washington, DC: National Academy Press.

Himes, John H. and William H. Dietz. 1994. "Guidelines for Overweight in Adolescent Preventive Services: Recommendations From an Expert Committee." *American Journal of Clinical Nutrition* 59:307-316.

Hirschman, Charles. 1996. "Studying Immigrant Adaptation From the 1990 Population Census: From Generational Comparisons to the Process of 'Becoming American'." Pp. 54-81 in *The New Second Generation*, edited by A. Portes. New York: Russell Sage.

Hirschman, Charles and Luis Falcón. 1985. "The Educational Attainment of Religio-Ethnic Groups in the United States." *Research in Sociology of Education and Socialization* 5:83-120.

Hogan, Dennis P. and David J. Eggebeen. 1997. "Demographic Change and the Population of Children: Race/Ethnicity, Immigration, and Family Size." Pp. 311-27 in *Indicators of Children's Well-Being*, edited by R. M. Hauser, B. V. Brown, and W. R. Prosser. New York: Russell Sage Foundation.

Idler, Ellen L. and Stanislav V. Kasl. 1991. "Health Perceptions and Survival: Do Global Evaluations of Health Status Really Predict Mortality?" *Journal of Gerontology* 46:S55-65.

Jasso, Guillermina. 1997. "Migration and the Dynamics of Family Phenomena." Pp. 63-77 in *Immigration and the Family: Research and Policy on U.S. Immigrants*, edited by A. Booth, A. C. Crouter, and N. Landale. Mahwah, NJ: Lawrence Erlbaum Associates.

Jasso, Guillermina and Mark R. Rosenzweig. 1986. "What's in a Name? Country-of-Origin Influences on the Earnings of Immigrants in the United States." *Research in Human Capital and Development* 4:75-106.

Johnson, Timothy P., Jared B. Jobe, Diane O'Rourke, Seymour Sudman, Richard B. Warnecke, Noel Chavez, Gloria Chapa-Resendez, and Patricia Golden. 1997. "Dimensions of Self-Identification Among Multiracial and Multiethnic Respondents in Survey Interviews." *Evaluation Review* 21:671-87.

Kao, Grace. 1999. "Psychological Well-Being and Educational Achievement Among Immigrant Youth." Pp. 410-477 in *Children of Immigrants: Health, Adjustment, and Public Assistance*, edited by D. J. Hernandez. Washington, DC: National Academy Press.

Kao, Grace and Marta Tienda. 1995. "Optimism and Achievement: The Educational Performance of Immigrant Youth." *Social Science Quarterly* 76:1-19.

Kaplan, Mark. S. and Gary Marks. 1990. "Adverse Effects of Acculturation: Psychological Distress Among Mexican American Young Adults." *Social Science and Medicine* 31:1313-19.

Kaplan, Sherrie. 1987. "Patient Reports of Health Status As Predictors of Physiologic Health Measures in Chronic Disease." *Journal of Chronic Disease* 40:27S-35S.

Klecka, William R. 1980. *Discriminant Analysis*. Beverly Hills, CA: Sage Publications.

Klein, Jonathan D., Karen M. Wilson, Molly McNulty, Cynthia Kapphahn, Karen Scott Collins. 1999. "Access to Medical Care for Adolescents:

Results form the 1997 Commonwealth Fund Survey of the Health of Adolescent Girls. *Journal of Adolescent Health* 25:120-30.

Kleinman, Arthur. 1986. *Social Origins of Distress and Disease.* New Haven: Yale University Press.

LaFromboise, Teresa, Hardin L.K. Coleman, and Jennifer Gerton. 1993. "Psychological Impact of Biculturalism: Evidence and Theory." *Psychological Bulletin* 114:395-412.

Landale, Nancy S., R. S. Oropesa, and Bridget K. Gorman. 1999. "Immigrant and Infant Health: Birth Outcomes of Immigrant and Native-Born Women." Pp. 244-85 in *Children of Immigrants*, edited by D. J. Hernandez, Committee on the Health and Adjustment of Immigrant Children and Families, and Board on Children, Youth and Families. Washington, DC: National Academy Press.

Landale, Nancy S., R. S. Oropesa, Daniel Llanes, and Bridget K. Gorman. 1999. "Does Americanization Have Adverse Effects on Health?: Stress, Health Habits, and Infant Health Outcomes Among Puerto Ricans." *Social Forces* 78:613-41.

Lantz, Paula and Melissa Partin. 1997. "Population Indicators of Prenatal and Infant Health." Pp. 47-75 in *Indicators of Children's Well-Being*, edited by R. M. Hauser, B. V. Brown, and W. R. Prosser. New York: Russell Sage Foundation.

Larsen, Luke J. 2004. "The Foreign-Born Population in the United States: 2003." *Current Population Reports, P20-551.* Washington, DC: U.S. Census Bureau.

Leslie, Leigh A. 1993. "Families Fleeing War: The Case of Central Americans." *Marriage and Family Review* 19:193-205.

Lessard, Gabrielle and Leighton Ku, . 2003. "Gaps in Coverage for Children in Immigrant Families." *The Future of Children: Health Insurance for Children* 13(1):101-15.

Liang, Jersey. 1986. "Self-Reported Physical Health Among Aged Adults." *Journal of Gerontology* 41:248-60.

Lollock, Lisa. 2001. "The Foreign-Born Population in the United States: March 2000." *Current Population Reports, P20-534.* Washington, DC: U.S. Census Bureau.

Long, J. Scott. 1997. *Regression Models for Categorical and Limited Dependent Variables.* Thousand Oaks, CA: Sage Publications.

Malzberg, Benjamin and Everett S. Lee. 1956. *Migration and Mental Disease: A Study of First Admissions to Hospitals for Mental Disease, New York, 1939-1941.* Social Science Research Council.

Marjoribanks, Kevin. 1987. "Ability and Attitude Correlates of Academic Achievement: Family-Group Differences." *Journal of Educational Psychology* 79:171-78.

Markides, Kyriakos S. and Jeannine T. Coreil. 1986. "The Health of Hispanics in the Southwestern United States: An Epidemiologic Paradox." *Public Health Reports* 101:253-65.

McLanahan, Sara. 1988. "Family Structure and Dependency: Early Transitions to Female Household Headship." *Demography* 25:1-16.

McLanahan, Sara and Karen Booth. 1989. "Mother-Only Families: Problems, Prospects, and Politics." *Journal of Marriage and the Family* 51:557-580.

McLanahan, Sarah and Gary D. Sandefur. 1994. *Growing Up With a Single Parent: What Hurts, What Helps.* Cambridge: Harvard University Press.

McLeod, Jane D. and Michael J. Shanahan. 1996. "Trajectories of Poverty and Children's Mental Health." *Journal of Health and Social Behavior* 37:207-20.

Mechanic, David. 1980. "The Experience and Reporting of Common Physical Complaints." *Journal of Health and Social Behavior* 21:146-55.

Mechanic, David and Stephen Hansell. 1987. "Adolescent Competence, Psychological Well-Being, and Self-Assessed Physical Health." *Journal of Health and Social Behavior* 28:364-74.

Mendoza, Fernando S. and Lori B. Dixon. 1999. "The Health and Nutritional Status of Immigrant Hispanic Children: Analyses of the Hispanic Health and Nutrition Examination Survey." Pp. 187-243 in *Children of Immigrants: Health, Adjustment, and Public Assistance*, edited by D. J. Hernandez, Committee on the Health and Adjustment of Immigrant Children and Families, and Board on Children, Youth and Families. Washington, DC: National Academy Press.

Mendoza, Fernando S., Stephanie J. Ventura, R. Burciaga Valdez, Richardo O. Castillo, Laura Escoto Saldivar, Katherine Baisden, and Reynaldo Martorell. 1990. "Selected Measures of Health Status for Mexican-American, Mainland Puerto Rican, and Cuban-American Children." *Journal of the American Medical Association* 265:227-232.

Mirowsky, John and Catherine E. Ross. 1989. *Social Causes of Psychological Distress.* New York: Aldine de Gruyter.

Moscicki, Eve K., Ben Z. Locke, Donald S. Rae and Jeffrey H. Boyd. 1989. "Depressive Symptoms Among Mexican Americans: The Hispanic Health and Nutrition Examination Survey." *American Journal of Epidemiology* 130:348-60.

154   *References*

Mossey, Jana M. and Evelyn Shapiro. 1982. "Self-Rated Health: A Predictor of Mortality Among the Elderly." *American Journal of Public Health* 72:800-808.

National Center for Health Statistics. 2000. *Health, United States, 2000 With Adolescent Health Chartbook*. Hyattsville, MD: National Center for Health Statistics.

Nunnally, Jum C. 1978. *Psychometric Theory*. 2d ed. New York: McGraw-Hill.

Padilla, Amado M. and David Durán. 1995. "The Psychological Dimension in Understanding Immigrant Students." *California's Immigrant Children: Theory, Research, and Implications for Educational Policy*, edited by R. G. Rumbaut and W. A. Cornelius. San Diego, CA: University of California Center for U.S.-Mexican Studies.

Park, Robert E. 1928. "Human Migration and the Marginal Man." *American Journal of Sociology* 33:881-93.

Patten, Christi A., J. C. Gillin, Arthur J. Farkas, Elizabeth A. Gilpin, Charles C. Berry, and John P. Pierce. 1997. "Depressive Symptoms in California Adolescents: Family Structure and Parental Support." *Journal of Adolescent Health* 20:271-78.

Pawliuk, Nicole, Natalie Grizenko, Alice Chan-Yip, Peter Gantous, Jane Mathew, and Diem Nguyen. 1996. "Acculturation Style and Psychological Functioning in Children of Immigrants." *American Journal of Orthopsychiatry* 66:111-21.

Pérez, Lisandro. "The Households of Children of Immigrants in South Florida: An Exploratory Study of Extended Family Arrangements." .

Portes, Alejandro. 1995. "Segmented Assimilation Among New Immigrant Youth: A Conceptual Framework." Pp. 71-76 in *California's Immigrant Children: Theory, Research, and Implications for Educational Policy*, edited by W. A. Cornelius and R. G. Rumbaut. University of California, San Diego: Center for U.S.-Mexican Studies.

———. 1997. "Immigration Theory for a New Century: Some Problems and Opportunities." *International Migration Review* 31:799-825.

Portes, Alejandro and József Böröcz. 1989. "Contemporary Immigration: Theoretical Perspectives on Its Determinants and Modes of Incorporation." *International Migration Review* 23:606-30.

Portes, Alejandro and Rubén G. Rumbaut. 1996. *Immigrant America: A Portrait*. Berkeley, CA: University of California Press.

Portes, Alejandro and Alex Stepick. 1993. *City on the Edge: The Transformation of Miami*. Berkeley, CA: University of California Press.

Portes, Alejandro and Min Zhou. 1993. "The New Second Generation: Segmented Assimilation and Its Variants." *Annals of the American Academy of Political and Social Science* 530:74-96.

Przeworski, Adam and Henry Teune. 1970. *The Logic of Comparative Social Inquiry*. New York: Wiley.

Radloff, Lenore. 1977. "The CES-D Scale: A Self-Report Depression Scale for Research in the General Population." *Applied Psychological Measurement* 1:385-401.

Ross, Catherine E. and John Mirowsky. 1984. "Components of Depressed Mood in Married Men and Women." *American Journal of Epidemiology* 119(6):997-1004.

————. 1992. "Households, Employment, and the Sense of Control." *Social Psychology Quarterly* 55:217-35.

Rumbaut, Rubén G. 1994a. "The Crucible Within: Ethnic Identity, Self-Esteem, and Segmented Assimilation Among Children of Immigrants." *International Migration Review* 28:748-94.

————. 1994b. "Origins and Destinies: Immigration to the United States Since World War II." *Sociological Forum* 9(4):583-621.

————. 1997a. "Assimilation and Its Discontents: Between Rhetoric and Reality." *International Migration Review* 31:923-60.

————. 1997b. "Paradoxes (and Orthodoxies) of Assimilation." *Sociological Perspectives* 40:483-511.

————. 1997c. "Ties That Bind: Immigration and Immigrant Families in the United States." Pp. 3-46 in *Immigration and the Family: Research and Policy on U.S. Immigrants*, edited by A. Booth, A. C. Crouter, and N. Landale. Mahwah, NJ: Lawrence Erlbaum Associates.

————. 1999. "'Immigrant Stock' Numbers One-Fifth of U.S. Population." *National Council on Family Relations Report* 44(2):8-9.

Rumbaut, Rubén G. and John R. Weeks. 1989. "Infant Health Among Indochinese Refugees: Patterns of Infant Mortality, Birthweight, and Prenatal Care in Comparative Perspective." *Research in the Sociology of Health Care* 8:137-96.

Sandberg, Neil C. 1974. *Ethnic Identity and Assimilation: The Polish-American Community*. New York: Praeger.

Sandefur, Gary D. and Jane Mosley. 1997. "Family Structure, Stability, and the Well-Being of Children." Pp. 328-45 in *Indicators of Children's Well-Being*, edited by R. M. Hauser, B. V. Brown, and W. R. Prosser. New York: Russell Sage Foundation.

Santisteban, Daniel A. and Victoria B. Mitrani. 2003. "The Influence of Acculturation Processes on the Family." Pp. 121-35 in *Acculturation: Advances in Theory, Measurement, and Applied Research*, edited by K.M. Chun, P.B. Organista, G. Marin. Washington, DC: American Psychological Association.

Schmidley, Dianne A. and Campbell Gibson. 1999. "Profile of the Foreign-Born Population in the United States: 1997." *Current Population Reports Special Studies, P23-195.* Washington, DC: U.S. Census Bureau.

Schmidley, A. Diane and U.S. Census Bureau. 2001. "Profile of the Foreign-Born Population in the United States". *Current Population Reports, Special Studies, P23-206.* Washington, DC: U.S. Census Bureau.

Schulz, N. 1983. *Voyagers in the Land: A Report on Unaccompanied Southeast Asian Refugee Children, New York City 1983.* Washington, DC: US Catholic Conf., Migrat. Refugee Serv.

Scribner, Richard and James H. Dwyer. 1989. "Acculturation and Low Birthweight Among Latinos in the Hispanic HANES." *American Journal of Public Health* 79:1263-67.

Shamsie, Jalal. 1995. *Troublesome Children.* Toronto, ON: Institute for the Study of Antisocial Behaviour in Youth.

Shek, Daniel T. L. 1997. "The Relation of Parent-Adolescent Conflict to Adolescent Psychological Well-Being, School Adjustment, and Problem Behavior." *Social Behavior and Personality* 25:277-90.

Short, Kathryn H. and Charlotte Johnston. 1997. "Stress, Maternal Distress, and Children's Adjustment Following Immigration: The Buffering Role of Social Support." *Journal of Consulting and Clinical Psychology* 65:494-503.

Shrout, Patrick E., Glorisa J. Canino, Hector R. Bird, Maritza Rubio-Stipec, Milagros Bravo, and M. Audrey Burnam. 1992. "Mental Health Status Among Puerto Ricans, Mexican-Americans, and Non-Hispanic Whites." *American Journal of Community Psychology* 20:729-52.

Sin, A., S. Kose, E. Terzioglu, A. Kokuludag, F. Sebik, and T. Kabakci. 1997. "Prevalence of Atopy in Young Healthy Population, in Izmir, Turkey." *Allergologia Et Immunopathologia* 25:80-84.

Sluzki, Carlos E. 1979. "Migration and Family Conflict." *Family Process* 18:379-90.

Sorenson, Susan B. and Haikang Shen. 1996. "Youth Suicide Trends in California: An Examination of Immigrant and Ethnic Group Risk." *Suicide and Life-Threatening Behavior* 26:143-54.

Sowell, Thomas. 1981. *Ethnic America: A History.* New York: Basic Books.

Srole, Leo, Thomas S. Langner, Stanley T. Michael, Price Kirkpatrick, Marvin K. Opler, and Thomas A. C. Rennie. 1978. *Mental Health in the Metropolis: The Midtown Manhattan Study*, edited by L. Srole and A. Kassen Fischer. New York: New York University Press.

Steinberg, Laurence. 1986. "Latch-Key Children and Susceptibility to Peer Pressure: An Ecological Analysis." *Developmental Psychology* 22:433-39.

———. 1991. "Parent-Adolescent Relations." Pp. L158-772 in *The Encyclopedia of Adolescence*, edited by R. Lerner, A. C. Peterson, and J. Brooks-Gunn. Garland.

Stonequist, Everett V. 1961. *The Marginal Man: A Study in Personality and Culture Conflict.* New York: Russell & Russell.

Suarez-Orozco, Carola and Irina L.G. Todorova. 2003. "The Social Worlds of Immigrant Youth". *New Directions for Youth Development* 100 (winter):15-24.

Sweeting, Helen. 1995. "Reversals of Fortune? Sex Differences in Health in Childhood and Adolescence." *Social Science and Medicine* 40:77-90.

Thoits, Peggy A. 1995. "Stress, Coping, and Social Support Processes: Where Are We? What Next?" *Journal of Health and Social Behavior* Extra Issue:53-79.

Tourangeau, Roger and Hee-Choon Shin. 1998. "National Longitudinal Study of Adolescent Health: Grand Sample Weight." Chapel Hill, NC: Carolina Population Center, University of North Carolina at Chapel Hill.

Trimble, Joseph E. 2003. "Social Change and Acculturation." Pp. 3-13 in *Acculturation: Advances in Theory, Measurement, and Applied Research*, edited by K.M. Chun, P.B. Organista, G. Marin. Washington, DC: American Psychological Association.

Troiano, RP, KM Flegal, RJ Kuzmarski, SM Campbell, and CL Johnson. 1995. "Overweight Prevalence and Trends for Children and Adolescents." *Archives of Pediatric Adolescent Medicine* 149:1085-91.

Vega, William A., Bohdan Kolody, Ramon Valle, and Judy Weir. 1991. "Social Networks, Social Support, and Their Relationship to Depression Among Immigrant Mexican Women." *Human Organization* 50:154-62.

Vega, William A. and Rubén G. Rumbaut. 1991. "Ethnic Minorities and Mental Health." *Annual Review of Sociology* 17:351-83.

Vilhjalmsson, Runar. 1994. "Effects of Social Support on Self-Assessed Health in Adolescence." *Journal of Youth and Adolescence* 23:437-52.

Walker, Zoe and Joy Townsend. 1998. "Promoting Adolescent Mental Health in Primary Care: a Review of the Literature." *Journal of Adolescence* 21:621-34.

Warner, W. Lloyd. and Leo Srole. 1945. *The Social Systems of American Ethnic Groups.* New Haven, CT: Yale University Press.

Waters, Mary. 1994. "Ethnic and Racial Identities of Second-Generation Black Immigrants in New York City." *International Migration Review* 28:795-820.

Waters, Mary C. 1996. "Ethnic and Racial Identities of Second-Generation Black Immigrants in New York City." Pp. 171-96 in *The New Second Generation*, edited by A. Portes. New York: Russell Sage.

———. 1997. "Immigrant Families at Risk: Factors That Undermine Chances for Success." Pp. 79-87 in *Immigration and the Family*, edited by A. Booth, A. C. Crouter, and N. Landale. Mahwah, NJ: Lawrence Erlbaum Associates.

Wickrama, K. A. S., Frederick O. Lorenz, and Rand D. Conger. 1997. "Parental Support and Adolescent Physical Health Status: A Latent Growth-Curve Analysis." *Journal of Health and Social Behavior* 38:149-63.

Williams, Ronald L., Nancy J. Binkin, and Elizabeth J. Clingman. 1986. "Pregnancy Outcomes Among Spanish-Surname Women in California." *American Journal of Public Health* 76:387-91.

Wong, Siu K. 1999. "Acculturation, Peer Relations, and Delinquent Behavior of Chinese-Canadian Youth." *Adolescence* 34(133):107-19.

Wytrwal, Joseph A. 1961. *America's Polish Heritage: A Social History of Poles in America*. Detroit, MI: Endurance.

Zambrana, Ruth E. and Victor Silva-Palacios. 1989. "Gender Differences in Stress Among Mexican Immigrant Adolescents in Los Angeles, California." *Journal of Adolescent Research* 4:426-42.

Zhou, Min. 1997. "Growing Up American: The Challenge Confronting Immigrant Children and Children of Immigrants." *Annual Review of Sociology* 23:63-95.

Zhou, Min and Carl L. Bankston III. 1994. "Social Capital and the Adaptation of the Second Generation: The Case of Vietnamese Youth in New Orleans." *International Migration Review* 28:821-45.

Index

Absence due to illness, 35, 48, 49
    51, 58-59, 61-62, 101-
    103, 107-113, 117, 121
Acculturation
    acculturative stress, 14-15,
    16, 24, 27, 37, 66, 71,
    77, 80, 120
    gaps in, 14-15, 24-25, 66,
    84, 101, 106, 116
Add Health, 31-33, 37, 39, 42,
    43, 44
Age at arrival, 36-37, 49, 51, 63,
    69, 122
American Psychiatric
    Association, 83
Assimilation
    process, 4, 7-9, 16, 28, 47,
    48, 57, 62, 64, 66, 73,
    84, 85, 100,102, 117,
    120, 123, 125, 127, 129
    segmented, 8-10, 12, 16, 21,
    27, 28, 47, 119, 127
    straight line or classical, 7-8,
    9, 10, 20, 21, 27, 28, 47,
    62
    theories, 7-12
Asthma, 19, 125

Bankston, Carl L., 10
Behavior problems (see deviant
    behavior)
Berry, John W., 10
Biculturalism, 10-11
Conditionally relevant variables,
    37
Contextual factors, 16, 25, 42-43
Deviant behavior, 20-22, 28, 34,
    38, 44, 48-49, 51, 54-
    55, 57, 62-63, 65, 83-
    88, 95-100, 103, 119,
    121-123, 127
Depression/depressive
    symptoms, 13, 23, 26,
    33, 44, 48-49, 50-51,
    53, 55, 57, 63, 83-86,
    89-93, 95, 99-100, 104,
    120-122, 126-129
Dixon, Lori B., 19
Epidemiological paradox, 17
Ethnic background, 2-3, 33, 37-
    38, 49, 53, 55, 61, 67,
    69, 75, 80, 87, 88, 91,
    93-95, 98-99, 103, 104,
    115, 117, 123
    Asian, 2, 3, 33, 37, 71

Black/African background, 3, 31, 32, 38, 42, 59, 62, 69, 71, 75, 80
Chinese, 21, 22, 23, 32, 33, 37, 71, 109, 126
Cuban, 18, 32, 37, 53, 59, 93-95, 100, 123
Filipino, 2, 33, 37, 53, 62, 80-81
Hispanic, 2, 20, 33, 37, 71
Mexican, 2, 17-19, 33, 37, 59, 109, 115-117, 123
Puerto Rican, 18, 32, 33, 37, 59, 98-99, 100, 123
Extended family, 38
Family process, 21-6, 40-42, 65-81, 119-120
Family structure, 22, 38
Gibson, Margaret A., 21
Gordon, Milton M., 7-8
Harker, Kathryn, 22, 23, 24, 66, 75
Harris, Kathleen M., 14, 18, 19, 20
Hispanic Health and Nutrition Examination Survey (HHANES), 17
Household income, 39-40, 104, 106
Immigrant/immigration adaptation, 4, 6, 7, 9, 11, 16, 27, 36, 47, 127
outcomes for youth, 3-4
population trends, 2-3
Implications of study, 5-6, 127-129
Independence in decision-making, 5, 22, 27, 40, 65, 67-69, 71, 73, 75, 77, 79-80, 85-89, 91-92 96-99, 102, 104, 106, 120-122, 128-129

Intergenerational conflict, 15
Language difficulties, 14, 37, 64
Limitations of study, 4-5, 124-125
Mendoza, Fernando S., 19
Mental health, 5-6, 12-6, 20-24, 27, 33-34, 53, 63, 83-85, 88-89, 99, 100, 103-104, 120-129
National Health Interview Survey (NHIS), 18
National Longitudinal Study of Adolescent Health (*see* Add Health)
Obesity, 18, 125
Ogbu, John U., 21
Overall health, 19, 35-36, 48-49, 51, 60-63, 101-103, 113-117, 119, 121, 123
Parental education, 40, 92
Parental expectations for education, 40, 70, 71, 73, 85-88, 96-98, 102-107, 112-113, 115-117, 120-121
Parental authority, 10, 15, 25, 66, 85, 101
involvement, 24, 27, 40-41, 65, 67, 69, 76, 77, 80-81, 85-86, 89, 102, 104, 106, 120, 121, 128
supervision, 21-23, 38, 66, 84, 102, 124
Parenting style (*see* family process)
Parent-child closeness, 23-24, 27, 41, 65-67, 69, 72, 73, 77, 79, 80, 85-86, 88-95, 99, 100-102, 120-121, 127-128

conflict, 15, 21, 23, 25, 41,
65-67, 69, 74, 75, 77,
80, 84-88, 96, 98, 101-
104, 106-107, 111, 113,
115-117, 120-121
relations (*see* family
process)
Perceived discrimination, 10, 14,
20, 125
Physical health, 12, 16-21, 27,
34-36, 53, 56-63, 84,
101-118, 121, 124, 126-
129
Physiological stress response, 34-
35, 44, 48-49, 51, 56-
57, 59, 61, 63-65, 101-
107, 113, 117, 119, 121
Portes, Alejandro, 26
Positive affect, 33-34, 45, 48-49,
51-53, 55, 57, 63-64,
83-89, 93-95, 99, 100,
120-123, 127-129

Poverty, 2-3, 9, 20, 22, 28, 42-
43, 53, 57, 59, 61, 67,
75, 77, 128
Problem behavior (*see* deviant
behavior)
Protective factors, 20, 85, 101,
128, 126
Race (*see* ethnic background)
Refugees, 26, 124, 125, 127
Risk behaviors, 11, 20, 84, 126,
127
Role reversal, 10, 15, 24, 66
Rumbaut, Rubén G., 23, 26, 66,
75
Sample, 31-3
Selection effects, 26-27, 123-124
Social support, 1, 5, 6, 17, 24,
26-27, 40-41, 65-69, 78-
79, 81, 87, 120
Theoretical perspectives, 7-12
Wong, Siu K., 21
Zhou, Min, 10

Printed in the United States
52643LVS00001B/385-432

9 781593 320973